We're Better Than This

YOUNG READERS' EDITION

YOUNG READERS' EDITION

WE'RE BETTER THAN THIS

MY FIGHT FOR THE FUTURE OF OUR DEMOCRACY

ELIJAH CUMMINGS

With Hilary Beard

HARPER

An Imprint of HarperCollinsPublishers

Library of Congress Control Number: 2021937257
ISBN 978-0-06-308155-0

Typography by Catherine San Juan
21 22 23 24 25   PC/LSCH   10 9 8 7 6 5 4 3 2 1

First Edition

To Baltimore—the city of Baltimore and
people of Baltimore.

To my parents, Ruth and Robert Cummings Sr.

And to our children, the living messengers to a future we
will never see.

CONTENTS

1

DON'T LET THEM MAKE US WAIT

"Elijah, don't let them make us wait anymore."

That's what my grandmother would say to me back when I was a younger man. For much of her life, my grandmother had heard white people tell Black people to wait—wait until things got better, wait for changes, wait and things would improve. But though she had seen progress, she hadn't seen Black people achieve equality.

"Don't wait anymore," she would tell me.

Since no one is guaranteed an infinite amount of time on earth, that's also a message I tell myself.

Nobody ever knows exactly how much time life will give

us. Nevertheless, time plays an important role in our life. We have to decide. Do we let the days, weeks, months, and years tick by unproductively? Do we let the clock run out as we watch other people take steps every day toward their vision for their life? Or do we use time wisely in ways that help us do well in school, provide support at home, contribute to our communities, develop a strong moral character, and work to achieve our wildest imaginings?

It's a message that I want to pass on to you. No matter what is going on in your life, even when it seems like you can't do anything, don't wait another day for someone else to do it. Take a step that moves your life toward your dreams. Do something that moves our society toward justice. Don't let any problem seem too big or too oppressive to overcome. Work on it over time.

Start.

Try.

Now.

You may not make it all the way to the exact outcome you imagined, but you will make progress, and where you end up will almost always be better than where you started out.

What's the best use of your time? What does your heart tell you that you should be working on? What actions would you take in your life if you knew that time was of the essence?

Start them now.

2

WHEN PRESENCE IS PRESENTS

Who am I? What motivates and excites me? How do I respond when life gets hard? What am I made of? These are questions you may ask yourself when you encounter the challenges and difficulties that are a natural part of life. They're hard to answer, but we have to look inside.

Today, many people know me as a successful congressman. I am not the kind of man who brags, but to understand what I'm about to share with you, it's important that you know who I am. I have been a member of the United States Congress for almost twenty-five years. That would be quite an accomplishment for anyone, but especially for an African American man who grew up very poor, grew up during the 1950s and '60s during the Civil Rights movement, and had to fight, uphill, and against the odds, to get there. As a congressman, I led the Congressional Black Caucus, an organization that helps make sure that the laws Congress passes are just as fair to Black Americans as they are to the white citizens of our country. And during some of the most tumultuous days of the presidency of our nation's forty-fifth president, Donald J. Trump, I served as the chair of the House Committee on Oversight and Reform, one of the most powerful in Congress, as I'll explain to you later.

But that isn't all of who I am, and it definitely isn't where I started off, or even who I was for most of my life.

I'm the product of those who came before me—my parents and grandparents—of those who surrounded me—my brothers and sisters—the people and places that shaped me, the streets I grew up on, and the lessons I lived and breathed, sometimes without even knowing it.

My parents were sharecroppers who left South Carolina and came north to Baltimore looking for a better life for themselves and their kids. Sharecroppers were Black people subjected to a form of servitude for decades after slavery had ended, when they were prohibited from owning property, and instead "rented" the very farmland that their ancestors had been enslaved upon, from white landlords, under unfair contracts that they could never pay off. Neither my mother nor my father had received more than an elementary school education. They could read and write, but they had never learned complicated math, science, or geography. Until they moved north, they never had indoor plumbing either. Instead, they had to go outside to use the bathroom in an outhouse, a small outdoor shack that has a toilet in it. But my parents taught us more than any teacher or class or school could. They imparted values and wisdom and experiences that never left us.

One of the Reasons

The wisdom I gained from my parents was rooted in their own upbringing during that era. I never knew my grandfather, but my father told me about him. In one particular story that stands out in my mind, my father was maybe eight years old, living in Manning, South Carolina. He was poor as could be, but smart as could be; nothing got by him. His father was a preacher (like my father became when he grew up and moved to Baltimore).

One Sunday, this grandfather I never knew was giving his sermon in the pulpit. And in the midst of preaching, in front of his whole church, he started not to feel well. He grabbed on to the pulpit, but then he fainted. Members of the congregation rushed to his side and tried to comfort him, but it was clear he was gravely sick.

So they lifted up his limp body, put him in a wagon, and pulled it down the dirt road to his little house. My father and his brothers and sisters ran alongside. He said his mother, my grandmother, held my grandfather's hand all the way home.

Somebody had been sent to town for a doctor, which they did in those days. Folks from the church put my grandfather in his bed and tried to make him comfortable. Finally, two doctors arrived—both white, one younger, one older—and they examined my grandfather. They poked here and there, feeling for fever, doing what doctors do. Then they walked out of the room together to discuss his condition and what could be done. My father waited on the porch, but he could hear most of the conversation.

The young white doctor said to the older one, "Doc, we have to get this man out of here." I assume he meant to a hospital or clinic, someplace that had better facilities and treatment. "If we don't," the young doctor continued, "he's going to die."

The older doctor said, "Don't worry about him. He's only a . . ."

My father, age eight, out on the porch, heard it all, even though they were whispering.

He's only a . . . The older doctor had said the N-word.

But he used the full word, the one we don't repeat because it is so offensive.

What the older doctor was saying was that he didn't see

my grandfather as a human being. He saw him as something less, someone who could be allowed to die—which is what would happen if he didn't get help. In those days, they didn't have heart surgery, but they had some ability to identify what was wrong, dole out heart medicines, and do other things that might save him. But he didn't get any of it. Because, in the eyes of that white doctor, he was only an N-word.

And that night, my grandfather died.

As I was growing up, my father would tell me that story, and no matter how many times he did, it was always just as painful for him because he knew that doctor didn't value his father's life.

When it came to his own existence, my father would say, "Lord, give me threescore and ten of life." I didn't know what a score was when I was a kid (it's twenty years and, if you do the math, he was saying that he wanted to live to age seventy), but my father got more than that. He made it to seventy-three. Still, for all of his life, that story of my grandfather never left him. And it's one of the reasons why my father became a strong advocate for making sure his own children, and his whole family, had proper health care. But even so, sometimes my family had to resort to home remedies to treat issues like asthma and pain from cavities.

The story never left me, either. I thought, *That's not right—somebody has to do something.* It's one of the primary reasons why I am so passionate in my belief that every American should have access to good health care, a network of resources that allow someone to maintain the well-being of their body and mind.

Life Lessons

When I was a child, during the 1950s and '60s, my father did low-wage, manual labor at the Davison Chemical plant (later owned by W. R. Grace). In those days, the bosses gave the Black workers the jobs that white workers wouldn't do. My father usually worked on the swing shift, 7:00 a.m. to 3:00 p.m. He did the demeaning, brutal, backbreaking work his foremen ordered: hauling drums, cleaning vats, carrying heavy loads, and getting filthy every day.

One of seventeen children, my mother did whatever she needed to do to get by all throughout her life, first to help her family and then later, our family. During my childhood, she took long bus rides out to the grand homes in Guilford and Roland Park, to clean houses of white people living in the nicer parts of the city, for $7.25 a day.

They both worked all week at these jobs, and then on weekends, they preached. That's right—we weren't just raised by two parents, but by two preachers. Later in life, they established their own church, the Victory Prayer Chapel, located near where we lived in Baltimore. I grew up in a house that was very religious. You couldn't dance or play cards. My mother lived to age ninety-two and never wore makeup a day of her life. We had to adhere to strict religion seven days a week. In reality, they preached all day, every day, in every room of our house, without calling it that. They gave us a strong moral foundation and taught us how to live.

Over the years, I've been asked why, given my background and values, I didn't become a preacher myself. People say I speak like a preacher, with that rhythm, cadence, and passion. I often use the words of the scripture. I look to God for guidance. I have, on occasion, even acted as a preacher. But I didn't become one because, by the example my parents set for us growing up, I knew you had to be perfect; a truly perfect person. And I am far—very far—from perfect. I am human, flesh and blood, passionate and vulnerable. So though that doesn't fit well with being a preacher, I think it enables me to reach out to people with human weakness and needs and help them.

Even today, I strive to live up to my parents' example that provided me with such a solid foundation. I remember that every day when my father came home from work, he had a ritual he would follow. He'd park his car, sit in it, and not come in the house. He was one of the few people in my neighborhood who had a car, and owning it was a point of pride. No matter how cold it was in the winter or hot in the summer, he'd just sit there, quietly, all by himself, in a world of his own, in front of our little row house near where Oriole Park is today.

For a full hour.

We kids wanted our dad to come inside but we knew better than to bother him. Years later, he told me what he was doing out there. Our father was letting go of the day's racial humiliations he experienced at work, allowing the anger and the pain to subside, giving the venom of insult and disrespect time to leave his body and mind before coming inside to his family.

He would not bring that negativity or bitterness into his home.

I never forgot that.

Later in life, I wrote him a letter because I wanted my father to know, before he left this earth, what his example meant to me. I told him that he was the most important figure in my life, providing for our family as best he could, never raising his voice to my mother. I told him I wanted to live my life as well, and as fairly, as he had.

We talked about what it was like at that job at the chemical plant, and he described the way he was treated—the disregard, degradation, and insults.

"I was called everything but a child of God," he said to me about the place where he worked.

That's why my father sat in his car. That's why he let the poison drain before facing his family. Following his example, to this day, I try not to let an insult or affront prevent me from dealing with adversaries. Like him, I sit in my car—figuratively, not literally—many times a day or a week or a year, and that enables me to pursue sometimes seemingly impossible tasks.

My mother had a major impact on me as well. Though she, too, had very little formal education, she was probably the smartest person I ever knew. She cleaned homes, took care of other people's children, prepared their meals, and then, at the end of an already long day, she came home to raise *her* seven children—Robert, Retha, Diane, Carnel, James, Yvonne, and me. Every night she then did the same tasks for our family that she had done all day for the family she worked for. As she cared for us, she passed on profound lessons as casually as putting dinner on the table or wiping a dish or waving to a neighbor. Life lessons just came out of her naturally.

Our family lived for each other, with each other, learning from each other, and protecting each other. My parents set examples for their children, and we, the kids, did our best to follow their lead and set examples of our own.

Presents Enough

My older brother, Robert Jr., was a huge reader, with walls of books, books, books. Reading wasn't the most popular thing to do back then among kids of our age or where we lived, but Robert didn't care. He read and absorbed and learned about life beyond our block and neighborhood. Robert's example rubbed off on me. I figured there must be something in those books worth knowing since they were taking up so much of my brother's attention. I didn't read nearly as much as he did, which would be almost impossible, but I learned the wonderful places books could take you and the worlds and possibilities they could open to you. Eventually Robert got a paper route to earn some extra money. So I did, too.

My older sister, Retha, taught me and looked out for me. For instance, if someone in the neighborhood wanted to beat me up, she was my protector, always looking out for little Elijah. I never forgot that. I held it inside and called on it later, whenever I'd encounter difficulty and need a boost of encouragement.

Though my parents had very little education, and modest jobs, they lived a life that led their children to achieve more. To get the education they never had. To see where it could take us. Robert became a lawyer; Retha and Diane are both nursing administrators; Carnel built a successful painting business; James served in the air force and now works in cyber security; my baby sister, Yvonne, performs research on how breast cancer affects African Americans; and I have reached some of the highest levels of the United States government.

My mother and father also raised us to be close to each other. That was family.

When we were growing up, some years were better than

others, and some not so good at all. In good years my parents would manage to scrape together money to buy nice Christmas gifts for us kids, but there were other years when they couldn't. One of those not-so-good years was when the workers at W. R. Grace, where my father was employed, went on strike. A strike is when workers stop working in an effort to pressure the management to improve their pay and working conditions. But back then going on strike also meant not getting paid. So our father told us in advance not to expect much in the way of gifts from Santa. As children, we thought, how could Santa let us down? We just didn't want to believe it. But on Christmas morning, when all of us kids came into the living room, we didn't see any wrapped packages. Not one. Any hopes of skates, games, baseball bats, or puzzles were gone.

My father sat in his favorite chair and watched us, with a sad look on his face. My mother sat next to him, with the same sad expression. We looked up at Daddy and in his hands were toothbrushes, one for each of us. Toothbrushes? Naturally, being kids, we couldn't help but feel let down, and I guess our faces showed it. But he didn't allow us to be disappointed. He explained again that this was a difficult time for our family, but it was still Christmas.

After giving each of us our toothbrush, he said, "You will not understand this now, but you will understand it later. My presence in your life is presents enough."

My presence in your life is presents enough.

He was speaking not only for himself, but for my mother, too. Having people who love you being there, in body and in spirit, is the greatest gift a child could have. You can't wrap that up and put a bow on it. You may not appreciate it on Christmas, but you can feel gratitude in your life, no matter what your family looks like, and whether or not the people who love you are related by blood.

The toothbrush our father gave us was a symbol, a token, something small that we needed. Having someone who loves you there with you—that is the real gift.

The bond of our family was unbreakable when things went well. And even more so in times that tested us. So no matter who raises you—or even if you're fortunate enough to have another type of mentor who spends time with you, like a teacher, youth leader, coach, or member of the clergy—the power of love and feeling of family can overcome all sorts of obstacles and deprivation.

One Regret

Yet, if I have one regret over my lifetime, it's that as an adult, my own family life has been imperfect.

I'd been raised to believe in the unbreakability of family, and that's what I carried into my first marriage so many years ago. We were married young—very young—but we had a beautiful daughter, Jennifer, who is now grown and doing wonderful things with her life. I've taken her to Congress, to the White House, to meet presidents. Nothing makes me prouder than to say that Jennifer Cummings is my daughter.

But the honest truth is, my marriage to her mother did not work. I can't say it was my wife's fault. Or mine. I can only say it was not meant to be. But how is that possible? It didn't fit the model I was raised with—the unbreakable family—and it took me a long, long time to finally face that reality. I had to reconcile that sometimes two people—two good people—are not intended to live under the same roof.

Later I had another daughter, Adia, an aspiring artist, photographer, and videographer. Both of my daughters followed my lead and prodding by going to Howard University. Both have made me so proud. Each came from a different time and place in my life. Each is bonded to me forever.

So are my brothers and sisters.

But on many occasions, I have put caring for my larger family—neighbors, constituents, the people of Baltimore— ahead of my biological family. My siblings, even as adults, have a tradition of monthly dinners, on the second Sunday of the month. When I met my now-wife Maya, I hadn't attended much. I knew they loved me and admired the work I did—my calling—but we had all just grown apart. Well, *they* hadn't, but I had.

Maya encouraged me to change that, to reconnect with my siblings, to restore the bonds that had been so strong when I was growing up. She and I began to attend, and it was wonderful for everyone. Reminiscent, warm, funny. Maya learned a lot at those gatherings. Like all of our nicknames. I wasn't called Elijah inside the Cummings family. Early on, my brother James nicknamed me Bobby . . . which made no sense since we had another brother named Robert . . . but it all made sense to us, and we laughed and relived stories that only we knew and shared.

Those suppers ended up being some of the most important moments in my life, and I hope in Maya's. She had grown up with traditions like that and knew how important they were. She even urged me to share hosting of family holidays at our house—Thanksgiving and Christmas. I treasure those times—they're the source of sustenance for me.

My mother had a stroke at age eighty-nine. She was frail and failing, but she did not spend one moment, not a single moment for the next two years, without one of us by her side. For two solid years there was a family member in the room with her. We didn't discuss it or plan it; we just did it. We were there until the day she left us. As family.

What I learned over a lifetime—and it has taken a lifetime—is that family may change, family may look different depending upon whose door you knock on and when, but the principles of family remain unbreakable. Faith, love, support, commitment, compassion, hard work, purpose, standing up for each other, and forgiveness.

Now that I've told you a bit about the people who have helped me become who I am, what about you? Where are you from? Who are the people who love and care for you? What drives you? When you look inside of yourself, what personal qualities have your loved ones passed down to you? Who and what are you made of?

3

HAVE NO LIMITS

When I was born, we belonged to the Mount Moriah Baptist Church, made up of mostly folks like us, from South Carolina. One of those people was Maggie Woodlaw, a friend of my mother, who became my godmother. In those days, members of the church often helped a family raise the kids, because nobody had much, but together folks could help take care of each other. Maggie was the woman who told my mother and father to name me Elijah. She'd read the story of Elijah, the prophet and miracle worker in the Old Testament of the Bible. Elijah was a messenger of God's word. For some reason, she felt that name was fitting for this new little baby.

When I was little, I hated my name. Kids would tease me, singing the old song "Oh Eliza, little Eliza Jane . . ."

As a young boy, I would have preferred a plainer, simpler name like my brother James or my father, Robert . . . anything but Elijah. But I went to church and, over time, read the biblical stories. I learned that Elijah stood up for the worship of God over the pagan deities, and God performed miracles through Elijah, one of which was said to be raising the dead. Elijah appears in many of the world's sacred texts—the Old and New Testament of the Christian faith; the Jewish Talmud; the Muslim Quran; the Book of Mormon; and the scriptures of the Baha'i faith. He was God's messenger to so many different people.

Elijah wasn't a plainer, simpler name. It carried real meaning. Eventually, I came to appreciate it. In fact, it is a humbling burden to carry. I am not a prophet. I do not perform miracles. But I try to live up to my name and legacy, to stand up for justice, to bring about change, to make people's lives better. I have also tried my best to listen for God's instruction and use my voice to speak truth even when the truth isn't popular.

Today many people just know me by Elijah, my first name. They don't know me as Mr. Cummings or Congressman. Just Elijah. They call out to me on the street. They send letters addressed, *Dear Elijah*. They greet me in church or on my way to work. They do not see me as a prophet, of course, but as someone who cares about them.

I do like to say I am a man of faith—not blind faith, but spiritual and human faith. I attend church every week that I am able, but God is not a once-a-week activity for me. I am, in every sense, spiritual. I feel I can discern the spirits of other people. If I cannot feel someone else's spirit, I tend to keep my distance. When I do feel it, I am drawn to those people.

Each morning, I follow a ritual of listening to gospel music, which grounds me and helps me prepare for the day. I pray for guidance, meditate on what to say, and then speak according to what I believe God has said to me. I try to do what God has told me to do. I am a man of great and abiding faith in the spiritual and religious sense, but also in the personal, hopeful, human sense. I have faith that things can get better. If . . . *if* . . . we put together the will and ideas and intentions to make them better. And if we don't, no amount of faith will fix things.

We Could Take Off

My faith helps me to be optimistic.

When we were little kids, some weekends my father would say to us, "Clean up, put on your nice clothes, and get in the car. We're going for a ride."

He'd take the whole family to what was then called Friendship Airport (it was later renamed Baltimore/Washington

International Thurgood Marshall Airport), to an area where anyone could watch the planes take off and land.

"Where do you think that one is going?" he'd ask as he'd point to a plane that was taxiing on the runway. Or he'd see one coming in for a landing and say, "Guess where that one is coming from."

We'd make up stories about the passengers going to visit family, or friends, or off to do business. Going to New York or Miami or Los Angeles or Paris. Anywhere they wanted to go.

Anywhere we could imagine.

It was exciting for us just seeing those big birds soaring into the clouds, going as far as our minds could take them. And nobody liked it better than my father. He told us he and my mom would never fly. They didn't have the money or even places to go. But he'd say to us kids, "You will, you'll fly. Someday. Mark my words. You'll be flying."

He carried that faith; he was optimistic. Then we'd look up at the sky again and dream where *we'd* be going. New places to do new things. Back then, I would envision it, very literally, a trip. Yes, someday I'd get on a jet, strap on my seat belt, sit back, and go off to another city or country.

When I was much older, I realized what my father had been teaching us.

He was telling us we could do whatever we wanted. We could soar, take off, have no limits, change the world.

That was flying. Not tied to the ground, not held back, not restricted by who society thought we could or could not be. Soaring.

You, too, can go wherever your imagination carries you. Just be sure to look at the airplane over your head and picture its path. Think about where you'd go, if you had no limits, if you could change the world.

Have faith and be optimistic.

Yes, you can fly.

Where would you like to go?

4

THE KEY TO SUCCESS

In our house, after God, came education. Right after God. But just because my family placed the highest of value on education—and emphasized over and over how it could transform your life—that didn't mean it came easy to me.

No, education was extremely arduous. I almost gave up so many times.

When I was in grade school I struggled, so they put me in classes labeled "special ed." Special education involves redesigning the lesson plan to educate students in a way that addresses their unique needs and learning differences, as individuals. There's nothing wrong with that. But I realized very soon that in this school, "special" was their way of saying "slow" or "behind the other kids" or "less demanding" and definitely "less interesting." Instead of loving school, I was frustrated, stymied, and discouraged. It was like wanting something that was just out of reach. But as I thought about the other students in my class, it became clear to me that we weren't the problem. The problem was that the school didn't know how to reach kids with different learning styles or who needed help catching up.

"Elijah, you don't look happy sitting here in class," my sixth-grade teacher said as he took me aside. "What's wrong?"

I guess my frustration showed on my face.

"I feel like a caged bird, like I'm all locked in," I told him, finally letting my discouragement out.

I was trying to express the fact that I wanted to learn more, but I couldn't. The classes wouldn't let me. My abilities and learning up to that point wouldn't let me. The teachers wouldn't let me.

I felt trapped.

Hungry to Learn

Thank God for my teacher.

He must have seen my potential, because he tutored me and gave me a path to learn—books to read on my own, after school and at the library, exercises, and homework. It was hard, doing all my regular schoolwork plus the extra work. I spent hours, long hours, at the public library, getting home late and doing more work.

Back then, most schools in Baltimore were segregated, either all Black or all white. Libraries were the only integrated places in my neighborhood. During those late afternoons, and sometimes late nights, the librarians noticed me there and would come over, see what I was studying, and offer help. I never forgot that—a lesson I learned while doing my lessons—that sure, there are some bad people along the way who will try to hold you back, but there are a lot of good people, as well. People who care.

Little by little I began to catch up and pretty soon the teachers saw my progress. They moved me into regular classes and I started to feel the rewards of school. Working together, that teacher and I made a change in me that altered my whole life. I became literally hungry to learn.

Education is a first step that enables change to begin. It is the road or the pathway to all transformation, so if you want to make a change in your life, learn, learn, learn. I knew that somehow, from my parents, from my siblings, from that sixth-grade teacher. I created my own saying, or mantra, that I would repeat to myself.

"Education is the key to success."

I wrote it everywhere: on my bedroom door, inside my schoolbooks, on papers that I'd aced. I don't know where I got it from, but I must have said it a thousand times in my own head, day in and day out. It was my obsession. I wanted to be a good kid, I wanted to be strong, I wanted to escape poverty, I wanted to get ahead (to where, I didn't know yet), I wanted my parents to be proud of me, I wanted to see more, and I wanted to be more. And I had to fight poverty, racism, segregation, and other barriers to get there.

And by the grace of God, the safety of my parents' home, the foundation of religion, changes in our society, some guidance, some luck, my own intuition, and whatever else was within me, I got to where I am today. Education, in one form or another, got me here.

Education is the key to success.

More Determined Than Ever

My father would say there's no such word as "can't" in your vocabulary. I wasn't allowed to say, "I can't do it." I couldn't even think it.

But I remember once when I was in middle school, we had a counselor who would call students into his office and ask how things were going and what you wanted to be when you finished school. I admired lawyers, from what I'd seen and read and heard about them. I even had a life-changing experience with one named Juanita Jackson Mitchell, which I will tell you about a little later. I pictured them to be smart leaders who helped other people get through life. So I told this counselor I wanted to be a lawyer.

The counselor looked at me and smiled politely, like people do when they think you're naïve and don't understand the "real world."

"Why don't you aim a little lower?" he said. "Maybe you should be a teacher."

In other words, he thought I couldn't do it.

I was discouraged, deflated, like the air had been knocked out of me. I didn't realize until much later that not only was he saying I wasn't good enough or smart enough to be a lawyer, but he was also saying that being a teacher was a second-class career, which it is not.

When I went home, I told my mother the story.

"Never let anyone define you," she told me. "Never!"

I won't ever forget the fury in her eyes and her voice. It stayed with me forever. That probably made me more determined to be a lawyer than anything else that ever happened to me. That was my fuel for the next few years—the drive to prove the counselor wrong.

I've passed that message along to many people, and to every graduating class I've ever addressed at a commencement ceremony, and there have been more than I can count. Education is the key to success, regardless of what some person tells you that you can or cannot be.

I went on to attend City College High School in Baltimore, which was highly competitive, all boys—Black and white—and one of the best schools in the state or the country at the time. I had to take several buses to get there, all the way across town from where I lived. It was probably eight or nine miles, though it took literally hours to get there. But it was okay because it was my ticket to college and to becoming a lawyer.

I had to do it. The way I saw it, I didn't have a choice. I just had to.

No Such Word as "Can't"

I'm not bragging but I didn't just do well in high school, I thrived. I was the president of the senior class. I graduated near the very top of my class. I had come a long way from my days in special ed and I was breathing the fresh air of my love of education.

I was flying like the planes I used to watch at the airport.

I went on to attend Howard University in Washington, D.C. While I was there, I just kept at it, saying and living my mantra—education is the key to success—becoming president of my sophomore class, and earning my key to Phi Beta Kappa, the nation's most prestigious academic honor society.

Man, I'd never imagined that a little kid from South Baltimore, from sharecropper parents, could do that, but my parents thought so, and they were right.

From there, I was accepted into law school at the University of Maryland. I was one driven student. When everybody went on weekend breaks or vacations, I studied.

I had my own little routine that started on Friday nights.

I'd get some Chinese food, a carton or two, and head to the library at about six thirty. From then until midnight I'd study, reading and rereading legal cases, doing the questions, looking up answers. Libraries had been my second home since those days of special ed. After studying, I'd head home to get some sleep. The next day I'd do my wash and get ready for the coming week. Then I'd go back to the library from two in the afternoon until six, and then see my girlfriend at night, maybe go to a movie or have dinner.

On Sunday I'd go to church and unwind, but just a little, then return to the library until seven or eight at night. Most of the students wouldn't do as much as I did. They'd study enough to get by, but I was a man with no alternative. I was on a mission! This is what I was here to do, my destiny. No distractions. Nothing to throw me off course.

And nothing did.

In those days there were limits on the number of Black people who were permitted to go to law school and how many would be allowed to pass the bar exam, the test that allows you to enter the legal profession. I did both.

When I became a lawyer, my middle school counselor—the one who told me to aim a little lower—well, he came to me as one of my very first clients.

Never let anyone define you. Your education is the key to success. And there's no such word as "can't."

5

NO MATTER WHAT SACRIFICE

When I was young my family rented a small house in South Baltimore. With two parents and five children, we were jammed in tight.

But when I was about ten years old, my father informed us that he and my mother were buying our family a house. He explained what buying a home meant. In our rental, he told us, any time we wanted to hang a picture, paint a room, lay down carpet, or put up a front porch light—anything—they had to ask the landlord. But my parents wanted their own "piece of America" and to "pass it down" to their children, as the American Dream. Because of the advances being made during the Civil Rights movement at this time, more Black people could now participate in, and be a part of, the American dream. Our civil rights provide us with political and social freedom and equality. They include things like the right to vote, to obtain a public education, to get a fair trial, and so on—rights our founding fathers had promised to land-owning white men from the very beginning—but which, during much of our history, Black Americans didn't have. For instance, during segregation, I wasn't allowed to walk in the front door of most white-owned stores or try on clothing or shoes. Even in my hometown of Baltimore, I was forced to sit in sections of buses and trains that white people designated as being for "Negroes only." The relentless and courageous push by Black Americans and our allies during the Civil Rights movement helped to transform our society so that Black people could participate more safely and freely. Many of these changes took place when I was a teenager, during the 1960s—and they helped transform our society into one in which all people, regardless of their race, religion, gender, or other personal characteristics—had equal rights. At least on paper, that is. We struggled—and still struggle— to make equal rights and equal justice a reality.

So my parents set a goal of owning their own home and, as a family, we practiced the discipline we needed to get there. Discipline requires self-control, curbing your behavior so you can achieve a result. You choose to either participate in or abstain from certain activities consistently in order to accomplish something important to you over time.

In this case, my parents saved every dime they could and cut back on spending. They prayed. As a family, we had to make these sacrifices together. My father and my mother explained that for us to afford to buy our own house, we wouldn't be able to get much that Christmas. Instead of resenting it, or complaining about it, we children rallied around it. We were excited. We were proud. We wanted to be part of it.

Eventually, my parents managed to scrape together enough money to buy a house in Edmondson Village, on Baltimore's West Side. It was just a little bigger than the house we rented and not too far away. But this one was ours, our own home. Owning a home was the reward of discipline—self-discipline, family discipline, and faith discipline.

No Matter What Sacrifice

Our new house wasn't just a house, it was a dream come true. Our American dream. An answered prayer.

My brothers and sisters were so excited about it that we got together and decided to use all of our money from running errands and delivering papers and groceries to surprise our parents on Christmas with things for our new house. We didn't ask them what to get; we just went to a local place called John's Bargain Store and bought what we thought we'd need—lamps, dishes, bathmats. Then we hid all the presents at a neighbor's house. On Christmas morning, our parents were shocked; I mean they couldn't believe their eyes. That was a good Christmas, and I think of the lessons from it often.

Though that holiday season was memorable, what happened, and what it stood for, was not out of the ordinary in my growing up. As I've explained before, that's just how we lived as a family—for each other, with each other, learning from each other, protecting each other. My parents set examples for their children. My brothers and sisters set examples for me, and I did for them. I also think that the purchase of our home showed that my father was a natural leader. He led us to understand the importance of having our own home, and got us to rally around it. I hope I get some of my leadership skills from him.

Discipline was never in short supply in our house. If you made a promise, you kept it. If you set your mind to do something, you did it. No matter how long it took. No matter what sacrifice it involved. You treated your family with respect, especially your parents. And if you didn't do what you said or show respect, there were consequences.

When one of us kids was out of line, we heard about it, or worse, felt it. In those days, a whipping wasn't uncommon. After the age of ten, I don't remember any of us getting spanked. By then we knew better. A look or a word from my father—which, in our eyes, may as well have been the voice of God—was enough to do the trick.

It's not that we were scared of our parents. Discipline isn't fear. Discipline is doing what's right. Our parents were open with us about everything. No one in the family was afraid to share anything with each other.

That's just what it was like growing up in my house—the house my parents bought for our family. No complaints, no fear. Just sacrifice, discipline, and a whole lot of love.

A Path to Follow

The discipline I was developing would come in handy when I was in the tenth grade. We were required to take geometry. It was probably the most challenging course I had ever taken at that point in my life. Each night, the instructor would give us at least ten, sometimes more, very difficult problems for homework.

There were evenings when I would spend literally hours on one problem. A few I'd eventually crack, while others, no matter how long I tried, I just could not figure out. I'd go to school the next morning frustrated, still thinking, still confused. The instructor would then ask one of my classmates who had solved the problems to work out each one on the blackboard. I had labored long and hard, sometimes without any success, but I was always excited to see the solutions, to see what steps I missed in my efforts, to see where the answer was hidden.

The second a classmate arrived at the part of the problem where I'd gotten stuck, I would experience one of those "aha" moments and feel chills down my spine because I finally saw what I was doing wrong. Most important, I knew what to do next time. If I had to solve a similar problem in the future, I would have a path to follow—what to do and what not to do.

I also realized that if I had not tried so hard to solve the homework assignment, seeing a classmate work the problems out on the blackboard would have meant very little to me. If I had given up, as lots of students did, I wouldn't have cared about the right answer. It made me think about so many kids who give up on studying and school altogether. They may never get to feel that aha moment.

For me, this wasn't just a lesson in geometry. I learned how important it is to stick with a problem until you figure it out. It's what learning is all about, and getting joy, real joy, out of finding an answer.

Try Until I Find a Way

I have always been willing to work hard, even in the face of discouragement. It's one of my strengths. But learning geometry gave me a new gift. If ever I fail in my efforts to accomplish a goal—a test, a job, a case, an election, a congressional vote—I always do what I learned from geometry class. I try to figure out what I did wrong, what I failed to do, or what I missed, like what I did when I watched my classmate solve the problem on the blackboard. Then I attempt the problem again and again until I find a way through it. I did this all throughout school, and I even do it now, as a congressman, whenever I fail to persuade a colleague or adversary.

I believe every one of us should set goals—problems to solve, things to strive for. It may sound a little old-fashioned, but if you don't set a goal, you don't know how you're doing.

You can also have goals and demonstrate discipline in relationships.

My father had a goal to have a loving marriage and home. Every single Friday, on payday, he stopped on his way home and bought my mother a flower and a candy bar. He couldn't afford to buy her a dozen roses or a big bouquet, so he bought one flower. And one candy bar, a Baby Ruth because her name was Ruth. That's all he could do. One flower and one candy bar at a time, he showed my mother his love. It was a small gesture, but years later, after he died, if you mentioned the flower and the candy bar to my mother, she wept. It was everything to her.

Let yourself imagine what you want to accomplish. Then spend some time breaking your vision down into teeny-tiny steps that are easy to do. What makes sense to do first? Then what step comes after that? And after that, and after that?

Do something small that takes you closer to your vision, every single day, every single week. That's what my parents did to purchase our house. That's what we did to surprise them that Christmas. The nickels, dimes, and quarters we'd been saving added up to something really wonderful. That's the power of discipline.

One way you know how you're doing is by looking at your progress. Are you one step closer to your dream than you were yesterday? Good, keep moving forward. Are you one-quarter of the way there? One-third? Halfway? Almost finished? Feel proud of yourself for each task you complete. And don't be discouraged if you don't immediately reach your goals. Most of the time we won't get there on the first, second, or even third try. Don't call that failure, call it progress. Learn from your mistakes and approach things differently the next time. And if that doesn't work, come at it from another angle. Again and again, until your dream becomes a reality.

6

A SPACE IN MY HEART

Life with my family in our modest row house in Baltimore taught me the power of love. That kind of love, I learned, can extend out to the larger community.

Can you love a place like you love a person? Or even more so? Can you love your roots, your home, and your heritage? Yes, you can.

Baltimore is a place—not just city limits or boundaries, but a place and space in my heart and soul—that I didn't just grow up in, but that I love. *Love*. Not merely like, or care for, or feel attached to, but love. It's unconditional, painful, rewarding, wrenching, uplifting, and total—like love of family. In fact, it is love of family. It is my family.

As a representative of this great city, I get up every morning because of this place and these people. I go to bed each night thinking of what I can do tomorrow that I didn't get done today. It isn't something to be explained; it just is. It is part of me like my heart, mind, and organs.

For much of my adult life, it has been my love.

I do whatever I can do, seven days a week, for anyone and everyone in the 7th District.

I Promised I Would Help

Out of love for my community, during my first week as a U.S. congressman, I sponsored a job fair. As someone who represents a district with a high unemployment rate, I had promised voters I would help find them jobs. We recruited businesses committed to hiring people, invited folks who needed jobs, and put them together, hoping for a match. I know it sounds ambitious for my first week on the job, but the families in my district needed it and that's what I promised, so I did it. And I've sponsored an annual job fair ever since.

Out of love for my city and my people, I have given away money I didn't have more times than I can count—and more money than I can count. But it's always been well worth it.

One day, a few years into my congressional service, I met

a woman at a local wedding, an elderly, frail woman who was lugging around an oxygen tank bigger than she was. Her face had such a worried look that I asked her what was wrong. She said she'd been gone from home that day much longer than she expected and was running low on the oxygen that helped her breathe a little more easily. She told me about her medical condition and how she couldn't live without oxygen, but she couldn't carry any more with her because this tank was already too much to handle.

I asked her if she knew about a small, portable oxygen device you can plug in and recharge wherever you are. She said yes, she'd heard of it, and it sounded like a miracle.

"Well, why don't you get one and then you wouldn't be dragging this elephant around behind you?"

She asked me how much it cost. When I told her three thousand dollars, she just shook her head sadly. I know, that's a lot of money for air. But I couldn't leave her that way. A member of my office staff was sitting next to me at the wedding and I asked him for a pen. He knew what was going to happen next, and he tried to catch my eye to maybe get me to reconsider, but he also knew there was no stopping me. I reached for my wallet and took out a blank check I carry, asked the woman her name, started to write, and then stopped.

"If I give you two thousand dollars, can you come up with the rest?" I asked her.

She nodded, with tears running down her cheeks. I told her my staffer would help her order the device. She called me about two weeks later and I'll never forget her words: "I'm free." The phrase "the pursuit of happiness" from the Declaration of Independence went through my mind. I believe people are entitled to the pursuit of happiness. That's freedom.

While serving my community I also identified scholarships for folks living in the blocks of my district. I pushed legislation to help homeowners, to make buying a house possible and to prevent foreclosures—when people fall behind in their payments and lose their home—because homes keep families together. I guided young men into drug rehab programs. I found health care for pregnant young women. I persuaded busy lawyers to defend people who could not afford an attorney. I spoke at every high school and every college I could, in order to encourage young people to strive up, to rise up, to see what is possible.

To fly.

Not to leave Baltimore, but to take Baltimore with them on their journey. To come back and pay it forward to their communities.

I Could Relate

But as much as I love my community, some things remain that I cannot fix.

During the Great Recession that spanned 2007–2009,

many people in my district had been kicked out of their homes—most because they had lost their jobs and couldn't keep up with their monthly mortgage payments. Losing your job in and of itself is hard and can mean many things—not having enough to eat, having the electricity and gas cut off, not being able to go to the doctor—but it also meant that homes that families had been living in suddenly got boarded up. This made the neighborhood less desirable and the value of other people's homes decline.

When a person buys a home, that purchase is usually the biggest investment they will ever make in their entire life. Having watched my parents scrimp and save and sacrifice and pray to buy their first house, I knew how important home ownership was. I also knew that a home—whether it's a room, an apartment, a condominium, or a house—isn't just an address, a doorway, a space. And it isn't just shelter and refuge, though those are vitally important. A home carries an even larger meaning. It is a place for kinfolk. It is almost synonymous with family. So losing your home is like losing your place in life, your family's center. It can zap the spirit out of you.

When the Great Recession hit and so many people started losing their homes, I could not accept what was happening. So, my office held workshops to teach neighbors how to hold on to them, how to negotiate, how to save the places where their families lived. When we opened the doors to those sessions, man, you would not believe how many attended. They offered people hope in the face of loss.

By 2010 and 2011, while some people in America had gotten back on their feet, there were still a good amount who had not. Countless numbers lived in districts like mine, which were the last to recover.

What made me extremely angry was when I discovered how a lot of banks handled this, allowing some people to be exploited while others were not. It turned out that all over the country, including Baltimore and across Maryland, banks and brokers had made people of color, and women especially, pay higher payments, which were harder to keep up with and depleted what little savings they had. Rather than helping these people, bankers ignored them or just wrote them off as folks who should have never been able to own a home in the first place.

But the people who came to me for help, they didn't want a handout, they just wanted to be able to get through this storm.

Truthfully, I could relate to their struggles, and not just from my childhood. In the late 1990s, my mortgage holder started the process of foreclosing upon me—kicking me out of my house just like so many of the people in my community had been kicked out of their homes. I hadn't lost my job, but I had fallen behind by six months on my mortgage payments. I had bills—child support, medical costs, taxes—the same problems everyone faces at one time or another. These problems grow, little by little, until they're huge and seem insurmountable. I'd managed to scrape together the money I needed. Many people aren't so fortunate.

As a result of the Great Recession, I pushed my colleagues in Congress to look into the abusive behavior that banks and mortgage lenders were engaging in. I pushed for loans to be reduced for people who were qualified. I pushed for members of the military and their families to be protected from being kicked out of their homes. Surprisingly, I was met with a lot of resistance. Even still, my office, my staff, and I continued to push.

And we helped people save a lot of homes. But some we could not help, and it broke my heart. To this day, every time I see a boarded-up house, I think that could have happened to me or a member of my family. I fight so it doesn't happen in my city that I love.

Justice Is Love

The love I have for my people and my community also prevents me from letting injustice go unaddressed. In fact, in the words of the college professor, author, and activist Cornel West, "justice is what love looks like in public."

In April 2015, the Baltimore police arrested Freddie Gray, an able-bodied twenty-five-year-old African American, for allegedly carrying an illegal knife. They handcuffed him and put him into a police van, then drove him to the police station. Somehow, along the way he went into a coma, and then had to be taken to a trauma center. A few days later, he was pronounced dead. The cause of death was injury to his spinal cord.

There was immediate outrage. How could a healthy young man sustain injuries in a police van that would result in him going into a coma? How could his spinal cord be damaged on a short trip to the police station? What was the truth of what really happened?

Later we discovered that the officers hadn't put on his seat belt, a violation of department policies. Many people suspect the driver may have also given him a rough ride intentionally to bang him up in the back of the van. His death was another unforgivable wrong in a growing list of urban human tragedies. News organizations from around the world descended upon our community.

I was asked to deliver the eulogy at Freddie Gray's funeral and the words came from my heart.

"To mother Gloria and to the entire family, I want you to know we stand with you during this difficult time." I looked right at that grieving mother and spoke to her one-to-one. "You brought him home. You played with him. You watched him grow. You heard the first time he read something. And you went to your own mother and said, 'That boy can read.' You just watched him grow."

I touched my fingers to my lips to send love for Freddie to his grieving mother. Then I spoke to all the mothers and all the fathers about all the Freddie Grays.

"As I thought about the [news] cameras, I wondered, 'Did anyone recognize Freddie Gray when he was alive? Did you see him?'"

I asked that question "Did you see him?" because Freddie was like so many hundreds, or thousands, or more young Black men, who our society treats as though they're invisible. Expendable. Taken for granted. Seen only when there is a tragedy, an altercation, a police investigation, a news story.

I repeated it, "Did you see him?" and then once more, "Did you see him?"

Three times.

Because all too often we do not see them. See that they have people who love them, that they go to church, that they play on the football team, that they have interests and hopes and dreams. And we must. We must see them.

I picked up the memorial program and read from it: "It says Freddie joined the World Life Missionary Baptist Church in 2001, where he joined the youth line and was a junior usher. Did you see him? He loved church-sponsored events, the latest fashions, and sports. He played football with the Sandtown Wolverines. Did you see him?"

I repeated it again and again, angry and sad and heartbroken. The question we must ask ourselves. I want the world to see our young Black men and women. Now. Not when they're headlines, but when they're here and alive and trying to create a life for themselves. I kissed my fingertips again for Freddie and his family.

"I've often said that our children are the living messages we send to a future we will never see. But now our children are sending us to a future they will never see," I closed. "There's something wrong with that picture." Why didn't we see him in life? Why don't we see so many in life?

After the funeral, I asked the public, the neighbors, and the media for calm and for justice. Love in action, love in public.

What's at Stake

Months later Freddie's death was ruled a homicide and several of the officers involved were charged with manslaughter. But legal actions against them ended in dropped charges, mistrials, and acquittals.

Before the officers could be charged, from April 18 to the 28th, the streets were full of angry, upset, untrusting folks. People marched. Crowds chanted. It was mostly peaceful, though emotions ran high. Some bricks were thrown. Some windows were broken. The city was on the verge of exploding. And no wonder. People felt they had been betrayed. The question was, what would they do with that anger and betrayal?

The mayor declared a curfew of 10:00 p.m. Night after night, I went out into the streets trying to keep the peace. I understood that if one bullet was fired, the city could blow up. But I thought, and hoped, I could help keep the calm by talking to the police as well as the folks who could create some serious problems. Why me? Well, I personally know a lot of people. These were my neighbors. This was my neighborhood. I live only five blocks away from Penn and North, an intersection that became the epicenter of the nightly unrest.

The very first night, I saw a man I knew, a young guy named John, who was kind of a leader. It was about 9:30, only a little before the 10:00 p.m. curfew.

"John, you need to go home," I said to him.

I could see he was mad. His eyes were on fire, he was agitated and walking fast through the crowds, shouting. I wasn't sure where his energy—powerful, and maybe dangerous— would take him.

"Congressman," he said, "I'm not going home."

I told him I didn't want him or any of the people out there, people he might influence, to get arrested.

"I can't do it," he responded. "I can't just walk away. Even if they arrest me."

I stood right next to him and reminded him that the last time I'd seen him he told me that he had two kids and a girlfriend, and a good job at the hospital. He took care of the kids at night when his girlfriend, their mother, was working.

He nodded, yes, that was still the case. So I asked him to consider what was at stake. Who was going to look after the kids if he got arrested? He said he didn't know but he had to be here, on the streets, right now, to deal with this unjust death. I knew how he felt but I couldn't leave him there. So I wrapped both of my arms around him and hugged him.

"I love you," I whispered into his ear. "I do not want you to get arrested." I knew that even though he might look brave or bold, like a leader, in front of his friends, it wasn't going to help him or anyone in the community if he let his anger get out of control. I kept holding him close and, in doing so, I could feel the bulge of a gun tucked in his belt. I said, "You know if you have a gun and the police find it, you're going to jail tonight." And then everyone would get more and more agitated. Who knows how many others had guns. Who knows what could happen. Again I said, "I'm telling you this because I love you."

"What did you say?" he asked me as though he almost couldn't believe it.

"I love you," I repeated.

And right there in the middle of the demonstration, John told me that I was the first man to ever tell him that. He went on to say that he sometimes felt like a man locked in a casket, trying to claw his way out. He didn't feel a lot of love. He and his friends and neighbors, when something like the Freddie

Gray thing happened, all felt caged and upset, thrashing out, looking for answers.

I know how he felt. I think I know how all the folks out there felt.

I promised him after this was over, I'd try to help him. And then I started singing—the spiritual "This Little Light of Mine"—quietly at first, and then building with more voices. "This little light of mine, I'm going to let it shine, let it shine, let it shine . . ."

Then John joined me singing. And pretty soon he was helping me tell people to go home.

The next night, I was walking the streets again, and I saw John.

"Here I am, reporting for duty," he said with a little salute. "We're going to make sure we get people home by ten."

I asked him why he was doing this. I was glad, but I wanted to know what happened, and why.

"The first thing you did was you showed respect for me," he replied. "And the second thing was, you said you love me." And he said there was something else, "That song . . . 'This Little Light of Mine.' I remember my grandfather, who'd been long dead, used to sing that song when I was a little boy in church." He kept going. ". . . I look at you as my grandpa, and I'm not going to walk away from my grandfather."

That's faith. And trust. And love.

I cried.

I face those situations all the time. Those moments are as important—maybe more important—than passing a bill in Congress. If you can reach one person, find a common path, then maybe you can change outcomes. Whether it's a brother on the streets or politicians across the political aisle in our democracy.

Trust. Just when you think it's not there, it can emerge.

Love is that powerful.

Too Big to Endure Alone

Sometimes loving a community means helping many people. Sometimes it means helping them one at a time. Sometimes the person you help isn't low income, or a minority, or someone people might expect would need help. It's just a person who encounters a devastating tragedy too big to endure alone.

Like Katie Malone.

Katie worked in my office, and one of her key jobs was helping young candidates for military academies—the Air Force, the Naval Academy, the military academy at West Point—get their applications in order, with the best possible presentation of their credentials, to compete for highly desired spots that could well change their lives. She threw herself into her job with a fervor. When one of those young men was admitted, it was as if Katie herself got in. To say I was reliant upon her is a vast understatement.

So when I found out about the fire that took her home, I was devastated. I learned about it almost by accident, as I went into a press conference at City Hall in Baltimore. Reporters came up to me and said they were sorry about my loss. What loss? I had heard about a tragic house fire on the radio in the car on my way, but had no idea it was the home of my staffer, Katie Malone. I learned the details outside City Hall. The home had been completely destroyed. Six of her nine children died. I wept profusely. I could not help myself.

The fire was all over the news. And immediately there was an outpouring of support, partly because the footage of me crying was shown over and over each time the story was told.

Congressman Cummings's staffer loses home to fire. Six children die.

Because she worked for an African American congressman, many people assumed Katie was Black. They assumed she was another "expected" inner-city story—single mother with nine children. But people quickly learned that she was a married white woman, who had nine children with her husband, and who held down a steady job. The public learned that tragedy knows no color or economics or preconceptions.

Loss of a home, loss of family, knows no boundaries.

I went to visit her in the hospital and when she opened her eyes and saw me, she asked, "What's happening with Jack?" I thought to myself, *Oh no, Jack must be one of her children.* Then she asked me about "Devon." And "Leo."

She explained that those were some of the young men she was helping with their military academy applications. Katie's life had been turned upside down, her loss was overwhelming, but she was looking out for others.

The public rallied around Katie and her husband and their kids. Donations were made. I gave her what I could. Others, many others, gave more. Her family was able to get a new home and try to start over. I do not take credit for the outpouring of support for Katie. My tears were shown and perhaps they moved people. I hope so.

Money doesn't make tragedies go away. But like it or not, it is a necessity. It can help. There is far too little of it for so many families. And sharing it can be an expression of love.

7

THE ONES WHO DELIVER

I have been a loner for most of my life. It's a bit of a contradiction because I come from a big family, and I reach out to, and affect, an entire community. But there is a very small number of people I will let get truly close to me. Though I don't have a lot of friends, those I have, I have for life.

People at work may change sides or aims or leave altogether. But friends, real friends, and that includes family members, are there forever if you take care of them.

"You've got to keep your friends," I tell my daughters.

"You don't want to ever be alone."

My mother taught me an essential life lesson about relationships. I can still hear her voice saying, "You teach people how to treat you."

When I first heard that, I thought, *What does that mean?*

I can't make someone be nice or give me respect or return my phone calls.

Or can I?

Maybe by the way I treat them—the way I act and react, what I say, whether I'm polite or demanding, kind or unkind, or the standards I hold them to—I can teach people to do right by me.

Teaching people how to treat you. It's very important.

To me, a close friendship requires trust. The way I look at it, there are two types, or two levels, of trust. The first is about honesty and integrity. This is when you ask yourself, *Is this person genuinely fair and do they act with integrity? Do they have strong values and moral principles?* If the answer to both questions is yes, then maybe that is a person to trust.

Maybe.

The other type of trust begs a different question: *Does the person do what he or she says they'll do?* It seems that should be simple. Intentions may be good, but results matter. If you say it, do it. But so many people don't do what they promise. They ignore their own words. The ones who deliver, who do what they say, those people will never let you down.

The first type of trust is special. The second is rare and precious. And finding someone who has both? Well, that's a person you should hold on to!

A Person to Trust

Bishop Walter Scott Thomas Sr., the pastor of New Psalmist Baptist Church, my church, is one of those few people who have earned both kinds of trust. He's more than my pastor; he's my friend and has been for decades. He is a charismatic, brilliant, sensitive man who has the unique ability to connect with people of all religions, ethnicities, and backgrounds. He is remarkable.

Bishop Thomas was studying economics at the University of Maryland when God called him to serve in the church. He then obtained both his master's degree and his doctorate of divinity. That's a whole lot of education, and it prepared him to lead his congregation of seven thousand people, have a nationally broadcast television show, *Empowering Disciples*, and write several books.

I brought President Bill Clinton to New Psalmist once, and he felt so at home and was so taken with Bishop Thomas and the church that he not only attended the service but stayed for the meal that followed. Then for hours afterward he engaged in conversation with Bishop Thomas to the point that we finally had to gently urge Bill to go back home to Washington, D.C. That is the powerful effect Bishop Thomas has on people. He has a tremendous ability to connect and bond with them.

I deeply trust Bishop Thomas. And I do not deeply trust many people. But once you've gained my trust, and I know I can depend on you, we are friends for life.

Bishop Thomas and I have developed both kinds of trust. I trust Bishop Thomas with my life. He trusts me with his.

How did we become such good friends? I have attended his church for thirty-seven years. For a lot of those years I was his lawyer and the church's lawyer. So I not only worked for the church on weekdays, but I prayed with the church on Sundays. Then, when I was elected to Congress, I had to give up my law practice and could no longer do the church's legal work. But the bishop and I could still counsel each other, seven days a week.

We all have things that we are good at and that we can share when our friends need someone to lean on. When I hear Bishop Thomas preach, it makes me want to be a better politician, to be as good at what I do as he is at what he does. It's like when I used to watch Michael Jordan play basketball—man, it was a beautiful thing to witness—and it made me want to be the Michael Jordan of the legal profession. I feel the same way when I see Bishop Thomas speak to his congregation. It inspires me to be the best I can be, to be more than I thought I could be. I rely upon him for spiritual things, for inspiration, and aspiration. In turn, Bishop Thomas can lean on me for political things; insight on law, rights, and justice.

At one point before the 2008 election, Bishop Thomas asked me who I was going to support as the nominee for president. The candidate who a minister supports for certain political offices can make all the difference in the amount of support that the public in that area gives the person. I said I hadn't determined that yet. He said, when you do, tell me, because whoever you support, I support. He reminded me that, to him, my knowledge of politics is like his knowledge of the Bible.

"Politics is your church," he would say, indicating that he respects my opinions and follows my lead politically just as I follow his on matters of faith.

Later, he reminded me that I supported Barack Obama way before he was even officially in the race. I just knew this man was destined to be our leader.

"If you trust him to lead, I trust you," Bishop Thomas told me.

I was the first person in Maryland, one of the first in the country, to come forward and stand with Barack Obama. That was hard for me because I had a close friendship with Bill and Hillary Clinton and I deeply respect both of them. But I had to make my stand. The bishop stood with me. His parishioners stood with him. And because Bishop Thomas is known all over the country by other pastors and their congregations, they all decided to back Obama, too. Then others began to follow.

That's trust. That's friendship.

That's what the brother—and I do mean brother—does for me. I can count on one hand, outside of my family, the people who I feel that way about.

During those times when my faith runs low—and it does for everyone—I sometimes turn to Bishop Thomas, and he to me.

"Elijah, borrow some of my faith," he has said when I have had doubts or despair about facing daunting odds of governing, family tragedy, or threats to our democracy. Whenever I'd encounter these challenges, I knew I could trust him with them. It wasn't just his faith in God that I was borrowing. It's his faith in the future, in turning the corner, in what could be . . .

When Baltimore almost erupted after the Freddie Gray incident, Bishop Thomas and I walked the streets tending to the people, together.

That's what a real friend does.

I remember a time, a dark moment in his life, when he had his own doubts and worries and he confided in me. "Bishop, take some of my faith," I told him, using that very phrase that he'd always use on me. He said he would.

You may notice that I didn't tell you the private information Bishop Thomas shared with me during that difficult moment in his life. That's because friends don't reveal each other's secrets. Keeping confidences is part of what builds a strong friendship.

Someone I Can Rely On

My chief of staff, Vernon Simms, is another good friend of mine. Vernon has been with me since the day I started working as a congressman on Capitol Hill. He had been the chief of staff for Congressman Kweisi Mfume, my predecessor, the person who held the job before me.

I liked Kweisi and our views often coincided. Still, I wanted my own staff, my own people, to start fresh with no allegiance to anyone else. But in those first days, I was overwhelmed with pressing matters of jumping into the job, one I didn't know much about. So I asked Vernon to help me out—just for a few days—with no obligation to keep him on. In fact, I almost promised him that he *wouldn't* be staying. But he did too good a job that I *had* to keep him. I came to rely on him almost immediately.

I learned fast that I could trust Vernon with anything. And I do mean anything.

One time someone stole my car and took it joyriding. I didn't even know the car was gone until a person in my district spotted my government license plates and called to tell me where the car had been left.

I asked Vernon to help me out. I gave him my extra car key, and he and another staffer, Debra Perry, took it upon themselves to go find the car. Once they found it, they called the police, but they took too long to come. Eventually, Vernon started the car and took off with Debra right behind, and together they returned the car to me.

I can trust Vernon with anything. Even my life.

My Extra Fulfillment

Sometimes friendship even turns into love.

I am a very private person, so romantic love is very hard for me to talk about. But that's what I found in my wife, Maya, my soul mate and the love of my life. Though we have only been married for eleven years, our connection seems like it has lasted for an eternity.

When Maya Rockeymoore and I first met on Capitol Hill in 1997, it was hardly romantic. It was all business back then. She was a graduate student working with the Congressional Black Caucus and had been assigned to work for a fellow congressman, Mel Watt. She was doing research on HIV/AIDS and I was among the first people to reply to her request to interview me.

Of course, I was very familiar with the issue. I cared about all of the people who were dying from AIDS and had been working diligently on finding solutions when Maya came to my office to talk. Back then, the disease, and the people who had it, experienced stigma, or shame and embarrassment, associated with it. In particular, it was stigmatized as a disease that impacted gay men and people who injected intravenous drugs, such as heroin.

"Stigma?" I responded when Maya asked me about it.

"That doesn't matter to me at all. It's about making sure that people can hold on to life." In her mind, that made me a transformational leader, at the forefront of a very tough issue, whose mind wasn't tainted by stereotypes.

For quite some time after that, I didn't see her much, but she was working on Capitol Hill, first for a congressional committee and then a congressman, and we would say hi when we saw each other. After a while, I had seen her so many times we became very friendly. Our conversations flowed easily, almost like we had known each other for a million years. When I'd see her, I'd sit next to her in meetings, at receptions, or in the House cafeteria. But there was nothing romantic, even remotely.

After a couple of years of knowing each other, I asked her out on a date. The date went well, but we just ended up being great friends for several more years after that. Months would go by, then we would talk on the phone for hours. Then not talk for months. Every now and then we'd go on another date. Five years went by before we finally connected romantically. Eventually, I asked if she would marry me.

Maya is *Dr.* Maya Rockeymoore Cummings, and I am always the first to emphasize the "Doctor" title. She has her Ph.D. in political science, is a policy consultant on issues of regional, national, and international impact, was the chair of the Maryland Democratic Party, is well-read, and worldly-wise. I love that she is incredibly smart. I am so fortunate to be married to my best friend, my very smart—book smart, school smart, life smart—best friend.

And she is my soul mate. That isn't just an expression. It means she is my extra source of fulfillment.

Bishop Thomas told me recently that he looks out at us in the congregation and he "sees a love that is rare." He said he sees it as we walk in and walk out, as we sit next to each other and hold hands, the way we lean over and talk to each other. I guess he sees it in things we don't even see ourselves. The pastor says it's all right there to view. Our love and our connection. Which almost embarrasses me, but I cannot argue with it. I just didn't know we were so obvious, like schoolkids.

She is with me everywhere, when she's there and when she's not. I hear her voice whispering in my ear. In the words of Bishop Thomas, "She feeds Elijah's soul."

8

THE GLUE IN OUR HOUSE

As far back as I can remember growing up, nobody in my family ever felt sorry for themselves. Now, that may seem strange since things weren't always good. In fact, we struggled a lot. Our family didn't have enough money. Ever. And racial discrimination was a fact of life. My parents worked hard and juggled multiple jobs. After a day of cleaning white people's houses, I recall my mother coming home and putting her feet in an Epsom salt bath, singing her prayers the whole time, then fixing our dinner and making sure we finished our homework. The next day, she'd wake up and do it all over again. Doing what had to be done for all of us. Yet she didn't complain about her feet or her back or feel sorry for herself. She knew that wasn't why she was put here on earth. She was here to raise a family and help people, and her hurting body wasn't going to stop her from her purpose.

Even though their lives were difficult, my parents knew that complaining didn't make things better. Doing something did. They lived by that belief and, as ministers, they built their churches on doing something, not wishing it so, or moaning about why it wasn't happening.

They said, and taught us, that when somebody needs help, you help.

Since my father was one of the few people in the neighborhood who had a car, he'd take people to the doctor or dentist or to apply for a job or visit a relative. When someone in the neighborhood was pregnant, my mother would take care of them, and then help deliver their babies, or take the mother to the hospital and look after the kids at home. We didn't have anything extra, but we gave what we had and more.

That was the glue in our house—giving.

And that meant feeling other people's pain and demonstrating empathy.

Empathy is the ability to imagine, understand, and share in another person's experience and feelings. In other words, being willing to imagine what it might be like to walk in another person's shoes, even, and especially, when they might be experiencing a hardship.

A Sliver of Hope

My parents weren't the only people I witnessed behave empathetically.

I got a job working for "Doc" Albert Friedman at Onnen's pharmacy in our neighborhood, doing whatever Doc said needed doing—unloading inventory, stocking shelves, and delivering orders. People came in for their prescriptions and Doc knew every one of them by name. He knew their medications and he knew what each person was suffering from. He knew how important those medicines were to each of his neighbors.

Doc Friedman also knew that sometimes people didn't have the money to pay for the prescriptions. So he just gave the medicines to them for free.

It wasn't good for business to give medicine away. In fact, it would cost Doc Friedman money every time he did it. But Doc knew that if you didn't get the insulin for your diabetes, or your blood pressure pills, or penicillin for your child's infection, you'd be in worse trouble than he would. He'd ask you to pay for it when you could, if you could. Plenty of times he never saw the money come back to him. He knew the moment he gave them the medicine that he likely wouldn't be repaid.

But Doc Friedman also knew that some things are more important than money. I have always remembered his kindness. He and my father shared the belief that all people should have health care. He shared my parents' values and behaved in a way that gave me a sliver of hope. Their willingness to sacrifice their time and money for others rubbed off on me. To this day, because of them, a lot of what I do for my community is prompted by the thought: *Somebody has to do something.*

One of my greatest strengths is to be able to feel other people's pain. I take it on as if it's mine. As a congressman, over and over and over, and year after year, I have seen similar stories repeat. I've witnessed grandparents dying, children suffering, families who can't afford medicine, people hurting. I saw it in my neighborhood, in my city, in the whole country. I can't tell you how many times I've had voters come up to me and tell me about an aunt who died because she had no insurance, a cousin who couldn't get an operation, a mother whose child died for lack of an antibiotic. People have given me letters and emails and folded-up notes, of terrible, awful, tearful stories that should just never happen.

So, I hurt for them. I have gone to church and prayed for people who couldn't afford to see a doctor, or go to an emergency room, or even purchase a pair of crutches.

Feeling people's pain is also one of my greatest weaknesses. How can it be both?

I carry the burden.

If I cannot soothe their pain, I feel I have failed and must keep trying and trying. I go to sleep at night thinking of other people's pain. And sometimes I cannot sleep because of it. That's just how it goes for me.

I don't complain about it. I want to do something about it. So, I get up the next day and try just that. To turn the pain into passion and the passion to purpose. My parents did God's work in the church. I try to do God's work outside the church.

Empathy is the ability to understand and share in another person's feelings. Compassion is being concerned for other people's misfortunes or suffering.

Who do you have empathy toward? Think about that person's life and consider what it might be like to walk in their shoes. How is your life similar to theirs? How does it differ? When has another person demonstrated empathy toward you? Next time you encounter someone going through something difficult, try exercising compassion and empathy in order to help them through it. Then consider how caring about the well-being of another person makes you feel. How does it feel when someone practices compassion toward you?

9

RESPECT THE STORM

No matter how good or caring we are toward others, all of us will face challenges, difficulties, and even hardship. Though today people call me successful, my life hasn't been easy. In fact, much of it has been hard. When I was eight years old, I learned an important lesson about managing life's trials and tribulations, which has helped me to this day.

It was icy that morning in Baltimore when my brothers and sisters and I went off to school, so slick that we had to be careful not to fall. Unbeknownst to us, on that same morning, one of our neighborhood friends was crossing the street when a car came through, driving too fast. The driver hit the brakes but slid on the ice and couldn't stop. He struck our friend and killed him.

We were at school when it all went down, so we had no idea we had just lost a dear friend. In fact, by the time we walked home, the sun had come out, it was warm, and the ice had melted. The storm had passed, but it left behind its damage.

Our family discussed what had happened to our friend, and at one point our mother warned us, "Respect the storm." Those were words I never forgot.

What did she mean when she said, "Respect the storm"? Act wisely when you see a storm—whether bad weather or one of life's many struggles. Do not behave foolishly or try to speed through it. Instead, use good sense. Behave accordingly. Move cautiously. Recognize the power and force of the difficulty you're experiencing and think about what type of lessons it's teaching you. And the kind of person you will be on the other side of it. After the storm is over. Because all storms, no matter how brutal, eventually pass. But the impact they leave on us, and the lessons we learn from them, could last forever.

Against the Odds

In 1994, when I was in my forties, I entered into a storm. I became very ill with a whole raft of symptoms. I was just in agony all over. The doctors performed every test imaginable.

At first, the diagnosis was elusive, but eventually an answer surfaced. It turned out to be thymic cancer, which is very rare and, frankly, almost always deadly. The cancer invades the thymus—a gland in your upper chest, behind your sternum and between your lungs—and prevents it from doing its job, which is producing the white blood cells the body needs to fight off infection. When you have thymic cancer, you become a magnet for disease.

The doctors told me the survival rate was low. They would treat me, operate on the tumor, give me radiation and chemotherapy, and have me participate in drug trials where researchers could try out new medications. But, the doctors said, I should approach life like I only had a few months to live.

So I have done just that.

For more than twenty-five years.

During that time, I've been under constant care at the Johns Hopkins Hospital—one of the most prestigious medical centers in the world, which happens to be located in my district. I've also been to the Washington Hospital Center, one of the top hospitals in the city, for chemotherapy and radiation. And I've received treatment at the National Institutes of Health (NIH), one of the world's most well-known medical research centers, where I was given a drug intended for kidney cancer, which I responded to for a while. The combination of treatments, the quality of medicine, the cutting-edge teams, the experimental drugs, have all helped me to defy the odds.

Ever since I got that diagnosis, I have gone about every day as if I have only months to live.

In fact, I was elected to Congress just two years later, in 1996.

Because I have such an intimate relationship with time, the very first speech I gave on the floor of the House was a recitation of a poem often quoted by Dr. Benjamin Mays, a civil rights leader, former president of Morehouse College, and inspiration to Dr. Martin Luther King. The poem is fittingly titled "God's Minute":

> *I only have a minute. Sixty seconds in it.*
> *Forced upon me, I did not choose it, but I know that I must use it.*
> *Give account if I abuse it. Suffer if I lose it.*
> *Only a tiny little minute, but eternity is in it.*

Just like a professional athlete toward the end of the game, I have lived much of my adult life playing against the clock. This is one of the lessons that I learned when I emerged from that storm.

Dreams Snuffed Out

Sometimes we face personal storms, other times we may have to deal with adversity with family members, friends, and other people we love and care about.

Even though my family has been strong, that strength has not made us immune to tragedy. While I was a congressman, my nephew Christopher died, or rather was murdered. Christopher was the son of my brother James, and his wife, Rosa, two wonderful people and parents. They lived in northern Virginia, in a happy, safe, tight-knit family with lots of love. No surprise, Christopher was one of those magical, charismatic children who steal your heart. He was such a good person; he started his own lawn care business at age thirteen, was very close to his father, and had always been a favorite of mine.

I knew I was a role model for him; he told me. I invited him to a picnic at the White House and he met Michelle Obama and had his picture taken with her. Man, was he thrilled. He got more and more interested in politics. At family gatherings, he'd pull me aside and say, "Uncle Eli"—that's what he called me—"tell me about your work." He was fascinated with what I did in Congress, with my life, and how I got to where I was. Christopher wrote a term paper about his heroes, Barack Obama and me. That's some high compliment.

When it was time for him to go off to college, I tried to convince him to go to Howard for undergraduate school like I did, told him what a good education I'd gotten, about the value of attending one of the HBCUs—historically Black colleges and universities—and how it impacted my whole life in terms of both knowledge and learning about my heritage as an African American. I talked to him about why I chose to go to the University of Maryland for law school, that my father said I should go there because his tax dollars paid for it and it was "our school."

But he didn't want an HBCU or a state school. He wanted to be where a lot of his friends were going, Old Dominion University in Norfolk, Virginia. Academically, he did very well, but evidently—and we never got real proof of this—he got involved with some bad folks, with some neighbors, not all college kids, during his junior year. Drugs may have been involved. One day Christopher's mother called me. Christopher had been shot. He later died. I had to deliver the news to my brother.

I reached James and told him to pull his car to the side of the road. My brother doesn't show much emotion, but I knew he'd fall apart. Losing a child—nothing can prepare you for that, nothing. The birth of a child takes your breath away. The death of a child takes your heart.

I was asked to deliver the eulogy at the funeral. I'd been to hundreds of funerals of young men, mostly Black men, who'd been shot down. Now this was one of our own family members. I talked about what Christopher had hoped to be and do, none of which would ever happen. His dreams had been snuffed out. He wouldn't follow in the steps of his uncle

Eli, or President Obama, or make his own, unique footsteps. It broke my heart to see that just taken away, gone, not to be any longer. Whatever Christopher imagined the day before would never emerge the next day. All that was there in the church was a body, a shell that looked like both the man he had become and the young boy he used to be. His family had sent him off to college, to get a degree and see what life held. He came back to us in a coffin.

What happened to Christopher? We don't know. To this day, Christopher's murder isn't solved. We will probably never know. Finding out the truth won't bring him back, but allowing it to go unsolved is a glaring injustice. He may have gotten himself involved in a bad situation and thought he could smile and charm his way out because he had an agreeable personality. His parents did everything right, but something still went wrong. Sometimes parents blame themselves even when there is no blame. Parents and kids are like a bow and arrow. You pull back, and back, as you raise them, trying to aim so straight, trying to put them on a good path, with love and affection, but finally you have to let go. And hope.

Every day is unsure. For all of us. I tell my young staffers, please be careful no matter where you are, whether you're at a community meeting, on your way home from work, out with friends during the weekend. There are good people hurt and killed by bad people every day.

My nephew was a brilliant young man, but I don't think he was so wise, street-wise. I'd have told him that if a guy comes in to rob you, put your hands up and say, "Take it." You're not getting out of that one with a smile or charm. Get out with your life, instead.

What came of Christopher's death? Pain. Unmistakable pain. But what else? This storm taught me how deeply I feel about gun law reform and mentoring youth.

If we're very still and open to it, the most devastating of storms can teach us the richest truths about ourselves.

What storms have you experienced in your life? What have they taught you?

10

HOW WE MADE HISTORY

At some point everyone will have an experience that has such a profound impact that it stays with you forever. I had one when I was eleven years old.

It was early in the 1960s. As we always did in the summer, the kids had all gathered at the neighborhood community playground center, where there was a small wading pool, with some recreation counselors to watch over us. After my sister had fed us breakfast, we'd go spend our day there, playing baseball or checkers, getting in the pool, or just hanging out with the other kids.

One of the rec leaders was a guy named Jim Smith. He was also involved with the NAACP, a legendary organization that has advocated for more than a century for Black people to have equal rights in America. Our little wading pool was no more than a few feet across and very shallow, maybe up to your knees. It was so small that it stayed filled with kids, side by side. You had to take turns, a half hour at a time, but on a hot day that was the only way we had to get cool.

Then one day in late August something interesting happened. A lady came and talked to us.

"How would you like to go to a real swimming pool, one with a diving board, an Olympic-size pool?" she asked.

We all thought that would be great, but how was it going to happen? She told us that there was a pool like that only a few blocks away, in a neighborhood called Riverside.

We deserved to go there, she said, and she was going to take us.

"You can swim to your heart's delight," she promised.

Those were her words: "to your heart's delight."

Later, I'd learn that the woman's name was Juanita Jackson Mitchell. She was a civil rights pioneer, the first African American woman to practice law in Maryland and a descendant of one of the signers of the Declaration of Independence. To us she was just the nice lady who was going to take us to a real swimming pool.

What Mrs. Mitchell did not tell us that day about the nice

pool was that it was racially segregated—only white people could swim in it.

No Black people allowed.

She and her colleagues at our rec center, Jim Smith and Walter Black, led us on a march to integrate the pool so that Black people could enjoy the water.

Mr. Black recalls that the leaders planned the event on August 28. On the 29th they went to visit the pool site. On August 30 and 31, and September 1 and 2, they led us on the first marches.

Toward Greater Equality

So there we were, a band of little kids walking down the streets of Baltimore, from a Black neighborhood to a white neighborhood. The communities were only a few blocks from each other, but they were also worlds apart.

Day after day, Mrs. Mitchell, Mr. Smith, and Mr. Black led about thirty of us, walking ten or fifteen blocks to get to the pool. As we walked, an angry mob of grown white adults yelled painful names, told us to go home, and threw rocks and bricks at us—little kids. One of those rocks struck me in the forehead and gave me a scar that I've worn the rest of my life.

The police watched and the newspapers took pictures and ran stories, but nobody stopped the angry residents . . . and nobody stopped us.

We all took one step forward toward the vision of greater equality.

Each day, we Black kids would swim in the Riverside Park pool. While we were there, white kids would push us in. Then we'd leave, with "neighbors" yelling racial epithets and throwing debris and bottles. I call them neighbors ironically. Yes, we all lived within blocks of each other, but they were hardly neighborly. They were the opposite, white people trying to keep us out of their neighborhood.

Tensions were high. After taking Sunday off, the organizers led us all back again on Monday, Labor Day, September 3.

That day someone called Mr. Black's associate, Lyle Roberts, the N-word. The hostility from the Riverside neighbors was escalating, so the police urged the NAACP leaders to let the police drive us all out of the neighborhood for "safety." At first, the leaders resisted but eventually agreed.

About that time, the Riverside citizens, as much as they tried to cling to their segregated white enclave, must have realized that we were just going to keep coming back, because they stopped huddling in their doorways and out in the streets, and stopped shouting and throwing rocks.

Just as Mrs. Mitchell promised, we all got to go to a "real pool," and as she said, we swam "to our heart's delight."

Even as little children we had a sense of victory—actually, victory *and* fear. We'd gone off to play every day, and through a frightening process, we ended up making history. Amazingly, nobody got seriously hurt.

The Power of Change

Baltimore stayed largely segregated for the next ten years, but that was the beginning, the root, of what would evolve into a massive upheaval in social norms. Old rules and practices and prejudices began, slowly but steadily, to change.

Because of our courage, the world became a little bit more fair.

For me, that was the beginning of wanting to become somebody who could make things change. I saw that Mrs. Mitchell and the other people who helped make racial integration happen were lawyers. That's what made me want to be a lawyer. Mr. Black, as well, became inspired by these events to go on to law school and then work for the NAACP. At that age, I was still learning what a lawyer was, what they actually did, but I saw what they could accomplish. I imagined them as young men and women who had the courage to walk up the streets and have people yell at them and be unafraid. To have little kids following them, trusting and believing in them. To make change happen. Oh my God, what a powerful force that could be.

Change.

Little Black children getting what only white children were once allowed to have. We were, after all, just kids, no matter what color, who wanted the same chances in life—the chance to swim in a pool, the chance to go to a good school, or live in a nice neighborhood, or see a better world. I wanted to be part of that change. And I have endeavored to do so ever since.

Many years later, I became a lawyer for folks in my neighborhood. For a couple buying a first home, for kids who wanted to go to college, for small businesses, for young men in trouble, for families about to be evicted, and for people battling bill collectors. I worked my way up to larger cases, but what my clients all had in common was the need for someone on their side to help them get what they were entitled to.

They needed help to get fairness. And I have pursued equity ever since.

The pool incident is the one that inspired me to become a lawyer, but it's just one of countless times that I have experienced racism's unfairness.

I felt it when my father came home from his work doing the "colored jobs." I felt it when my mother took the bus home from cleaning the fancy white homes north of us. I felt it when police arrested young Black men at double or triple the rate of white men. I felt it when Freddie Gray was killed. I felt it with every funeral I attended. I felt it when I saw people lose their homes. I felt it when I drove my car through a white suburb, where so many times a Black man driving a nice car draws the attention of police and, once stopped, he becomes more susceptible to being harassed, arrested, or perhaps even losing his life, even though the only thing he was trying to do was get to his destination. Yes, I felt the paranoia, worry, and fear that so many Black men feel when we're in situations where we know someone might consider us a threat. I felt it when I heard hateful names being slung at Black members of my community. And frankly, I felt it when racism wasn't spoken with words but still felt equally loud.

11

SEE WHAT IS POSSIBLE

When I began training to become a lawyer, racial quotas limited both the number of Black students who were permitted to go to law school and the number of Black law school graduates who would be allowed to pass the bar exam.

Because this quota system existed, I started my own course to tutor young African American law graduates—to guide and prepare them to take the Maryland state bar exam. With a small staff of Black and white attorneys, we tutored young lawyers-to-be to give them a better shot at passing the exam, and we improved the outcome dramatically. I didn't do it for money or notoriety or publicity. I did it because the odds were tilted against Black students without this type of mentoring. The system was unfair, so I set out to make it more fair.

What I didn't know was that some influential people were aware of what we were doing. Among them was Lena King Lee, a teacher and attorney. She called me to meet and talk. As only the third Black woman to earn a law degree from the University of Maryland, she understood the obstacles placed in Black people's path to keep them from becoming lawyers. She hadn't entered politics until age sixty. At the time she was serving in the Maryland General Assembly, where, back in 1970, she had founded the state's Legislative Black Caucus, an organization of lawmakers who fight to help ensure that Black Maryland residents actually experience the rights that the U.S. Constitution promises. The nation's Congressional Black Caucus was formed just one year later by a group of Black congressional representatives who had first come together during the 1960s to discuss their common concerns. I would go on to become chair of both the Maryland Legislative Black Caucus and the Congressional Black Caucus.

When we met, Lena Lee told me that after many years of service, she was going to retire. She had been looking for a Black female attorney to take her place but hadn't found the right person. Then she heard about my free bar exam course, researched me, and decided I should be the person who took her place in the General Assembly. In other words, she wanted me to run for political office—to take over her seat—as a Maryland state delegate.

"You'll do," she told me—high praise from a woman of high standards.

I'd had exactly zero ambitions of going into politics until that moment. But Lena promised that she would help me raise money, support me, and assist in getting my campaign off the ground. I needed this kind of advice and support, or I wouldn't stand a chance. She persuaded me that public service was my calling, our calling, and it must be done. In fact, she became my mentor. A mentor is someone who coaches or advises you in an area where they have more experience than you do; someone who believes in you and will help you move closer to your goals and dreams. These are great people to ask for advice, share plans with, discuss worries and fears with, and they can help you identify other people who can assist you or guide you to pick yourself up after you've hit a roadblock or fallen short of the goals you'd hoped to achieve.

It's Better to Try

Suffice it to say, in 1982 I won Lena's seat, which became yet another turning point in my life. For the next fourteen years, I served in the Maryland House of Delegates, all the while keeping most of my law practice going (state legislators don't make much money). Like Lena, I became chairman of Maryland's Legislative Black Caucus. I was also voted the House's speaker *pro tem*, the second most powerful position in that legislature. And as far as I was concerned that was it for my entire political career, but events intervened again.

While I was driving home from Annapolis, the state capital, one day in late 1995, I heard on the radio that a member of the U.S. House of Representatives, Congressman Kweisi Mfume, was leaving his position representing the 7th Congressional District. He would soon head the NAACP, a famous civil rights organization. That left his seat wide open.

I wouldn't have challenged Kweisi in a million years and I sure wasn't waiting for him to retire, since he was only a couple years my senior. Nor was I looking to run for national office. But some folks started talking to me, urging me, convincing me, and pretty soon I figured it's better to try, even if I fail, than to not try at all. There were seven candidates, including me. That lot eventually narrowed down, and I emerged as the Democratic candidate. I won again, beating the Republican candidate, in the regular election in November.

I, of course, prepared myself and did the work, but role models like my sixth-grade teacher; Mrs. Mitchell, Mr. Smith, and Mr. Black, who desegregated the pool; all the librarians who helped me with my studies; and mentors like

Lena Lee and others played an essential role in pushing me to see my own potential and to go for new goals and dreams.

Reaching Past Barriers

Mentoring has played such an important role in my life that, more than twenty years ago, I began the Elijah Cummings Youth Leadership Program, to mentor the next generation of young people in Baltimore, across barriers and racial and ethnic boundaries.

These young trailblazers, tenth graders, most Black or Brown, first go through a rigorous selection process, then a yearlong leadership development phase. They're mentored by leaders in Baltimore and Washington, D.C. Then they spend a full month in Israel, touring Jerusalem, Tel Aviv, Nazareth, and the Dead Sea, sharing the experience of living in another culture, one that survived the Holocaust, is under threat daily in the Middle East, and has nurtured its past and protected its future. In the third year, these young people put their experience to work back home, in the community service phase. They, in turn, mentor other kids—middle school children in our district—sharing and spreading what they learned, showing another generation how to reach out beyond themselves, past differences, to see what is possible.

In twenty years, we've sent more than two hundred young Black Americans from Baltimore to Israel, all from my congressional district. They go for free, the result of a contribution from Jerry Hoffberger, former owner of the Baltimore Orioles and a prominent Jewish philanthropist. And it was built on my own belief that we cannot, as Black Americans, progress without coalitions, and our greatest coalition partner has been the Jewish people in America.

The program has touched hundreds of lives; those who went, those they mentored, their families, and their neighbors. One hundred percent of those selected have graduated from high school and 95 percent have graduated from college. Many have gone on to achieve tremendous accomplishments in their chosen fields. The CNN weekend news anchor Victor Blackwell was one of the first selected for the program more than twenty years ago. It means the world to me to see folks from the leadership program thrive like this.

In areas where you are passionate or have interests or a vision, look for a mentor to advise and support you. Just as I mentored the young law students. Just like Lena Lee took a chance on me to fill her Assembly position. And just like the Elijah Cummings Youth Leadership Program pays it forward to promising youth. Look for people with more experience than you or organizations that can help you along your way. No one can succeed on their own.

Has anyone ever mentored you? If so, what was the experience like and how did it benefit you? Who do you know from your family, school, neighborhood, community, or beyond who might mentor you toward achieving your goals and dreams? How can you pay the good energy forward? Who in your life can you do the same for? Perhaps a friend, a younger sibling, or someone who looks up to you?

12

UPHOLDING DEMOCRACY

I believe there is an arc to each chapter of our lives, and those chapters all come together to create a larger arc—the story of our purpose and progress over a lifetime.

My life's journey has taken me from being a low-income kid, the son of sharecroppers, a special education student and someone who felt embarrassed about his name, to someone who loved school and excelled there, became a lawyer and advocate for his community, was elected to the Maryland state legislature, and served twelve terms representing his hometown of Baltimore in the U.S. Congress. In time, I would be appointed the chairman of the House Committee on Oversight and Reform, one of the most important committees in all of Congress. But I'm jumping a little ahead of myself.

God has put me on earth to serve.

For years I have had a recurring dream where I see myself running down a street lined with people.

One person shouts out, "I need a blanket," and I hand him a blanket.

"I need a cane," says another, and I hand her a cane.

"We need food."

"We need shoes."

As I run down that street, I hand each person what they need. I just keep running and running. To help others rise up—to find food, shelter, clothing, hope, and truth. That is my purpose. And it requires all of the values and character traits that my parents and life have taught me, and that I am sharing with you.

They Called Us Chattel

In 1996, I began my first term as a member of the United States House of Representatives, in Washington, D.C. My mother and father were there with me. My sharecropper, modestly educated, working two jobs, raising seven kids, weekend preacher parents lived to see me rise from South Baltimore to the halls of Congress. Though they didn't have very much education, though they worked difficult jobs and sometimes were treated poorly, their lives were about something bigger than themselves. Their lives had purpose and I was a part of it.

In the shadow of the Capitol, under the U.S. Constitution, in the company of my parents, I took the oath of office. That day, I saw my father weeping, openly, trying to wipe away his tears. I don't think I could remember ever seeing my father cry, so I asked him about it.

"Daddy, were you crying?" I inquired, secretly wanting him to lie, to say, "No, no, I was perspiring."

"Yes," he replied. "Yes, I'm crying."

"Why?" I asked him. "Because your son is now in the U.S. Congress?"

"This is a great moment, but that's not why I'm crying," he said. "I kept looking at your hand. I realized that the same blood that runs in your hand runs in mine."

I nodded.

"Elijah," he said, "isn't this the place where they used to call us slaves?"

"Yessir," I answered him, reflecting on our nation's ugly and contradictory history.

"Isn't this the place they called us three-fifths of a man?"

"Yessir," I answered him, as he referred to the language in the Constitution that counted enslaved Black people as three-fifths of a person when determining the number of representatives in Congress who would represent each state.

"Isn't this the place they called us chattel?"

"Yessir," I replied, as he referred to the days when many white people enslaved Black people, treating us not as though we were human beings, but instead as though we were property.

I'll never forget what he said next.

"When I see you sworn in today, now I see what I could have been if I had an opportunity."

Opportunity. My father and mother and their ancestors didn't have it. But it's all everyone needs to enjoy "life, liberty, and the pursuit of happiness," the inalienable rights that the Declaration of Independence promises that our government will protect.

Since I am African American, my ancestors were not immigrants, that is, people who arrived here seeking freedom in new lands. On the contrary, they had been free in Africa, then people enslaved and forcibly brought them to America. I am the grandson of African-descended people held as slaves. They did not come here for a better life. They were kidnapped, put in chains, packed in the bottom of boats, shipped overseas, auctioned off, kept in bondage, working not for wages but to build wealth for white families and to stay alive. My great-grandparents' ancestors were enslaved for two generations. My grandparents and parents were sharecroppers—I am the child of sharecroppers who migrated north for a better life.

My father and my mother overcame the tremendous adversity they faced and gave me that opportunity.

No, my father did not have the opportunities that I had in my life. He had been born in a nation whose Declaration of Independence promised that "all men are created equal" but during an era when white people who were in power were acting to ensure that it never became a reality for the nation's Black citizens. Still, my father's life, and my mother's, did have purpose, and that included providing for and raising their children, with the hope that we could have opportunities that they weren't able to access.

So even though many of my ancestors were enslaved, their lives had meaning. Part of their commitment included raising their children, part of it included participating in the fight for "life, liberty, and the pursuit of happiness," for equality, challenging the United States to become a "more perfect union."

Yes, part of my forebears' purpose included struggling to shape the world's first multiracial democracy. And I see that as an important part of my responsibility—to continue that fight.

We the People

Former U.S. attorney general Robert Kennedy—the nation's highest-ranking lawyer during President John F. Kennedy's administration—once said, "Democracy is messy. And it's hard. It's never easy."

A democracy requires the people who live in it to be

informed about how it works, its purpose, its most important concepts, to be active citizens, to protect it. We have rights in our democracy, such as freedom of speech, the right to protest, and the right to a free press, but we also have responsibilities. Our responsibilities include staying informed about what's going on, participating in our communities, being part of the democratic process—including voting—and defending the Constitution.

Our Constitution sets forth the collection of "rules" our nation follows, the basic principles that set the United States apart from the British monarchy we overthrew during the American Revolution back in 1776. We rejected the arbitrary rule of one person, a king or queen, who the people had not elected or voted for or agreed upon, but who had been chosen by birth and blood. We chose to rule ourselves. We chose, instead, to vote for our leaders.

So the first words of the Constitution, "We the people of the United States of America," are essential to our life and freedom every single day.

Our founding fathers chose a balance, or separation, of power, distributed across three branches of government that are equal to each other: executive, legislative, and judicial. The executive branch is the president of the United States. The legislative branch, Congress, is made of the Senate and the House of Representatives. The judicial branch consists of the Supreme Court and other lower courts.

This system of checks and balances exists to prevent one branch from having absolute rule over the others. In theory, this helps to keep each branch of government honest, from overstepping its role and failing to represent the desires of "we the people."

There's a lot in there that's important for us to understand: three branches, not one. Executive power to implement and enforce laws resides in the president, who is elected by the public. For four years at a time—not for life, like a monarch—to provide balance. Legislative power, that is, the creation of all laws, resides in Congress. Congress has two houses—an upper chamber called the U.S. Senate and a lower chamber called the U.S. House of Representatives—more balance. Judicial power resides in the Supreme Court—to rule on whether the law and the actions of the president are constitutional. Additional courts are established by Congress—again, more balance.

This deliberate system prevents one branch from over-powering any other. Our form of governance is designed to maintain the will of the people. Each of these measures is an attempt to create fairness.

So when one arm of government, say the executive, disagrees with another arm, the legislature, often the only resolution comes from the third arm, the judiciary. These ideas form the basics of civics—the study of the rights and duties of every citizen and the responsibilities of government.

It's important for everyone to understand them because democracy is very fragile. It takes a tremendous amount of effort to preserve and make it work. It's also important to understand civics if you are a public servant, meaning that you work for the government, either at the local, state, or federal level.

But democracy can be slow. Painfully slow.

When one branch does something another branch disagrees with, the process requires review by one of the other branches, according to the built-in checks and balances. It takes a lot of patience to do government work, especially to do it openly and fairly, with balance, and without the mandate of a king or emperor or dictator. To do it the way our founding fathers and the Constitution intended.

It's messy, it's hard, and it's never easy. But it works. In the words of Martin Luther King, "The arc of the moral universe is long, but it bends towards justice."

Fairness.

In other words, it may take a long time to get there, but eventually we usually do. Even in the areas where we're not there yet, by learning about how government works, learning who represents you, understanding the issues, asking if you can go with your parents when they vote, and registering to vote when you come of age, you can help us do better, become more perfect.

Now that I was a United States congressman, I was part

of that process, the legislative branch, a congressional representative.

Upholding democracy was now also part of my purpose.

One Voice, One Vote

In a representative democracy, the public votes to select who we want to stand in for us politically. Our democracy rests on the principle of one person, one vote. Everyone has a voice. To me, that is fair.

The ballot, the piece of paper or the electronic process people use to cast their votes, is the most powerful weapon in a democracy. Votes can change history. Votes can change who is in office, where we can live, where we can go to school, how much we can earn, who we can marry, how well our families and communities fare . . . life itself.

We should encourage everybody to vote, no matter their political beliefs. Our elections should be equitable. Everyone has a voice. To me, that is fair. So defending our democracy involves protecting the right to vote that so many of our ancestors shed blood for and fought hard to win.

Though our nation's founding fathers may have had fairness and freedom in mind when they established the United States, it's also true that they chose to set our society up in ways that were very unfair. Among other weaknesses, our nation, which was supposedly built on the notion of "liberty and justice," permitted Black people to be enslaved.

Injustice.

That tragic flaw is just one shortcoming that makes our country an "imperfect union." And though our founders introduced this flaw centuries ago, its effects are long-lasting, and it is our responsibility to right the wrong.

Another tragic flaw in our Constitution is that our founding fathers intended white men who owned land to be the only Americans able to vote. Women, people of other races, and even white men who didn't own land weren't allowed to cast ballots. And as you know, they counted Black people as three-fifths of a person when they decided how many representatives each state would have in Congress. Thankfully, the Fourteenth Amendment to the Constitution, which established "equal protection under the law," did away with the Three-fifths Compromise. But that still didn't make our nation equal or correct the flaws in representation.

But didn't Black men get the vote after the Civil War?

Yes, in theory.

The Fifteenth Amendment, passed in 1870, states: "The right of citizens of the United States to vote shall not be denied or abridged by the United States or by any State on account of race, color, or previous condition of servitude."

Voting is our right, not a privilege, as citizens of our country. But throughout history many Americans have had to fight to be able to vote.

For example, during and after Reconstruction—the era

between 1865 and 1877, after the ending of slavery, when the nation made its first attempts both to exist without slavery and to form a multiracial democracy—racist white people intentionally denied Black people the vote, passed laws to take it away, and used and threatened violence to keep them from even trying to vote. In thirty-eight states, North and South, state and local laws, customs, and practices known as "Jim Crow" legalized segregation, or the separating of people by race. These laws and conventions lasted well into the 1960s and were the reason my parents had been sharecroppers, and why I attended a segregated school, lived in an all-Black neighborhood, and participated in integrating the neighborhood swimming pool. Jim Crow laws also helped states prevent Black people from voting, by imposing poll taxes, literacy tests, and other restrictions upon Black Americans. Poll taxes were a fee Southern white people forced Black people to pay in order to vote, and they were usually too expensive for most to be able to afford. White people didn't have to pay this tax. A literacy test meant you'd have to prove that you could read. During slavery it was illegal to teach a Black person to read; afterward it took years for people who had been enslaved to learn. Oftentimes a paragraph of the Constitution would be used for the test, which few people of that era could read, no matter their race. And, again, white people weren't required to take it. Strategies like these, used to keep people—disproportionately Black and Brown—from voting, are known as voter suppression.

And by the way, the Fifteenth Amendment only applied to men, not women. White women wouldn't win the right to vote until the Nineteenth Amendment passed in 1920. Many Black women wouldn't win the ballot until the Voting Rights Act of 1965, which prohibited racial discrimination in voting. Until then, various methods to suppress the vote kept most Black women from using the ballot to represent their political interests.

Give Us the Ballot

The Voting Rights Act is not just another law to me. It is sacred. And it has been, to me and every person of color, since the day of its inspiration.

In 1957, when I was six years old, Dr. King gave one of his most historic speeches. Back then, because of tactics like poll taxes and literacy tests, Black people were still battling to be able to vote. Besides my parents, Dr. Martin Luther King was the most significant figure in my life and in the lives of all Black people. When he spoke, we heard him. On the radio, on television, in the newspapers, at rallies. He was our guiding light.

"Give us the ballot," he implored, exhorted, demanded, in that speech. I don't know if I remember from listening to it on the radio, watching it on television, from my mother and father talking about it at the dinner table, or just from hearing the story told over and over through the years, but those words have never left me. I knew it was a moment in time we would not forget.

"Give us the ballot."

In 1957, President Dwight D. Eisenhower proposed, and Congress passed, the first major civil rights legislation since Reconstruction. Remember, civil rights provide political and social freedom and equality—regardless of your race, religion, gender, sexual orientation, or other personal characteristics.

It also gave the judiciary branch power to protect the vote, to keep people from interfering with people's right to vote. In those days, that usually meant protecting Black people's ability to vote from racist white people who wanted to prevent that from happening.

This legislation, the Civil Rights Act of 1957, was later followed by the Voting Rights Act of 1965, which President Lyndon B. Johnson signed.

I can still picture the photograph of President Johnson handing the pen with which he signed the act to Martin Luther King, the man who would not rest until it became law.

The playing field still wasn't level, but with the stroke of that pen the nation became more fair, at least on paper. And it was possible because of the millions of people who, over centuries of time, took small steps forward toward creating greater equality.

The Voting Rights Act overruled the many legal barriers

that state and local governments had implemented since Reconstruction to prevent Black people from exercising their constitutional right to vote, which had been guaranteed by the Fifteenth Amendment. The Voting Rights Act opened the door for more Black people to vote, including Black women.

But not every politician wants to share power. Some know that the fewer people who vote, the fewer people they have to answer to, and the more power they retain.

With these kinds of ideas in mind, some members of government unfortunately engage in schemes to undermine the Voting Rights Act. Instead of ensuring people's right to vote, these politicians try to scare certain people into not voting, thereby limiting their power, rights, and benefits. Historically, the people they've tried to discourage from voting have been Black and Brown and young.

Today, some politicians want to make it easier to vote by encouraging strategies like automatically registering people to vote when they turn eighteen, turning Election Day into a national holiday so everyone has time to vote, and allowing people to start voting many weeks before the election. Strategies like these would help ensure that everyone's voices are represented and that our democracy reflects the desires of the people who live in it.

However, other politicians attempt to suppress the vote by redrawing the lines around voting districts to make some votes worth more than others, a practice called gerrymandering. Other approaches to voter suppression include purging names from lists of registered voters, imposing strict laws about the type of identification voters must present to cast their ballot and making it difficult and expensive to obtain that ID, preventing people who were previously incarcerated but have served their time and paid their penalty to society from voting, closing polling places so that there are fewer places to vote, moving polling places so they are harder to reach, shortening the hours that voting places are open, eliminating early voting, requiring college students to return to their hometowns to vote, and more.

The fact that so much of our nation's history involved denying the vote to so many citizens—and especially Black Americans—makes me all the more determined to fight for justice and equality in Congress.

Which brings me to our forty-fifth president.

13

JUST GETTING STARTED

In January 2017, Donald J. Trump became president of the United States. I received an invitation to his inauguration. Every member of Congress gets one, but not everybody goes. I didn't like the way, during his campaign, he made remarks that offended everyone from President Barack Obama and his wife Michelle, to a long list of Republican politicians. And it didn't end there. He went on to make offensive remarks about Mexicans, women, Muslims, immigrants, Black Americans, people with disabilities, the "Gold Star" families of military men and women killed while fighting for our country—the list goes on and on.

But I thought to myself, *This guy, whether I like it or not, is going to be the president of the United States for four years. I've got to represent the 700,000 people in my congressional district, no matter what. I don't know exactly what this president and I, as a legislator, can do together for the American people. But if there are things that we can agree on, I want to get them done for my constituents and for the country.* So I decided I wanted to go.

I knew I could get a lot of criticism for attending. In addition to disparaging so many American citizens, at that moment, Trump was in a dispute with a good friend of mine, the legendary civil rights leader and Georgia congressman John Lewis. If you want to learn about a courageous man and an American hero, John Lewis is a great person to start with. I went to John and told him that I wanted to go to the inauguration but would never do anything that looked like I was disrespecting him.

"No, Elijah, you should go," he said to me. He understood exactly why—that I needed to reach across the aisle in order to represent my constituents, the citizens and voters whose interests I represent.

With his blessing, my wife, Maya, and I attended the inauguration. We also attended the luncheon after the swearing in. It was a very exclusive event—we hadn't even received an invite to President Obama's luncheons. The lunch took place in Statuary Hall, a beautiful two-story chamber in the U.S.

Capitol ringed with life-size sculptures of important figures from American history. The organizers seated us at a table with some of the president's family, where we ate, listened to remarks from him, Vice President Mike Pence, and other dignitaries. During a lull in the program, Maya and I walked up to the head table to greet President Trump.

"I'm really glad to see you," he said. I guess that was partly because he thought Democrats, and especially African Americans, would stay away due to the many offensive remarks he had made. There were very few of either group in the room.

I used my brief time with him to talk about the high cost the pharmaceutical companies were charging for prescription drugs, an issue that was very important to me.

"They're getting away with murder, those companies," the president agreed. That's a quote. He said he wanted to sit down and talk about what we could do. Honestly, I was surprised, but I saw it as a sign that maybe we could cooperate.

A Pretty Good Start

Not long after the inauguration, I got a call from the president—directly from him—that he wanted me to come to the White House.

In fact, I became the first member of the Democratic Party to meet privately with Donald Trump. I met with him with genuine optimism. Caution, yes. But I had faith that two people from opposite worlds and perspectives could accomplish good things, even though we disagreed on some very important topics. Even though I am the son of share-croppers and Donald Trump is a real estate billionaire and reality television star, I believed that we could overcome our differences.

I invited Dr. Redonda Miller, president of the Johns Hopkins Hospital, to join me. I also asked Congressman Peter Welch of Vermont to attend. Both believe that prescription medications should be less expensive. Surprisingly, we had what seemed to be a wonderful conversation with President Trump. The person I am, the person I've always been, came out. And I thought the real him came out, too. I knew I was meeting with the president, but I didn't feel like I was meeting with someone who occupied such a prestigious position. I live in the inner city of Baltimore, and I'm used to people being very straight with me—no games. And that's how we talked . . . or so I thought. I don't know if it was just me being naïve, but I felt like I could reach him, that there was a level of mutual respect.

He asked me why I was so personally concerned about prescription drugs. I can remember my words. I told him I'd seen too many people die because they simply couldn't buy their medicine. To me, if you're sick *and* you don't have any money, it's downright cruel to say "there's nothing we can do." And even for people who make good money, if they're told they need to buy a medication that costs a thousand dollars per pill to stay alive, what may have seemed like a whole lot of money can quickly dwindle to nothing.

I know people who have faced that dilemma. They have to make a heck of a choice: Do they take away from their families so that they can stay alive? Or do they say, I can't put that burden on my kids or my wife or my husband, and then they die?

As I was telling him that story, a tear came to my eye.

"That's a real tear?" Trump asked.

I nodded.

"Yeah, Mr. President, it's real, man." I said it just like that. I felt like I was talking to a guy on my street, not the president. Just man to man. That's how we talked.

I then told him about the law Congressman Welch and I were drafting that would empower the federal government to negotiate prices with the pharmaceutical companies that sell the drugs. The president liked the idea. "Let's get it done," he said.

I thought, *Well, that's a pretty good start*; it seemed like a good note to end on.

Something Positive?

President Trump wanted to keep talking, so we did, just the two of us. At that point, I took the opportunity to get a few more things off my chest.

"Mr. President, why do you say things that are so mean?"

I asked, testing the waters. And then I went on. "The Muslim ban," I told him. "You don't need to do that. It seems like you're representing just the people that like you. Mr. President, you should represent everybody. When you talk about the African American community, when you call these areas 'dangerous,' when you talk about African Americans like we're all doing bad, like we're all in the ditch and can't get out, and we live in murder capitals, I wish you wouldn't do that, because it hurts us."

"You really mean that, don't you?" he asked.

"Yeah, I mean it," I said. "Mr. President, you're almost seventy, man, and I'm sixty-seven. It won't be too long from now that you and I will be dancing with the angels. Why can't we join together and get some things done, like lowering prescription drug prices, that will be good for everybody? If we're able to do something like this, you could become probably one of the greatest presidents that ever lived."

I started with "if"—*if* he could do something like this—and that was a big "if" because it meant he'd be doing something for everyone, not just his supporters, who would probably follow him to the end of the world. All he had to do was try to help the other people.

He said he liked that, and as I walked out of his office, he told me he'd be in contact with me very shortly.

Two or three days later, I got another call from the president.

"Congressman, I'm working on this thing. I'm going to see what I can get done," he told me.

I was hopeful, truly hopeful. What if we really started something positive?

The Unfolding Storm

Not too many days after I met with the president, I began to have health problems of my own. That April, after a long day on Capitol Hill, I felt like I couldn't catch my breath. I'd been working nonstop and just figured I was worn out, but it happened the next day and the next. Finally, I mentioned it to my wife Maya.

"Elijah, you're going to the doctor," she said. "You're going now."

So, we went. That tells you a lot about me and a lot about Maya.

The doctor checked me out—the usual questions, poking, tapping, breathe in, breathe out, stethoscope, listening to my heartbeat. Then he ordered an echocardiogram, a test of my heart. Turns out I had "aortic stenosis," a narrowing of the aortic valve, the largest artery in the human body. The narrowed artery was cutting off the flow of oxygen to the rest of my body, and that's why I was short of breath.

And that's also why it's so important to have access to good health care, which I do because I'm a member of Congress.

My physician said I was lucky. The surgical procedure to

fix aortic stenosis is quick, proven, and recovery is fast. They scheduled me for the next day. Still, I was realistic. I prepared two envelopes. One was a list of people to contact if all went well, to tell them not to worry, that Elijah's fine and will be back to work soon, so don't let anything slide. The other contained instructions on what to do if things did *not* go well—my wishes and funeral plans in detail in case I ran out of time.

Then I called my dear friend Vernon, my chief of staff. I asked him to meet me and Maya at the hospital. I gave the first envelope to him and told him if everything went as planned, to open it after the surgery and contact the people listed. I told him to give the second envelope to Maya if things did not go well, if the clock ran out. The following day, I had the procedure.

I was ready to feel better quickly, but my recovery stretched for months. To my surprise, I developed a very painful form of arthritis, called gout, where your joints can feel like they are on fire. My feet started throbbing, and pretty soon, I wasn't able to move. Several months later, I developed an infection in my knees that required surgery. Life slowed down. Work slowed down. I had never experienced anything like it. It reminded me that time on this earth is limited, finite, short. That I was coming face-to-face with my mortality. I would not be here forever. But with the help of physical therapists, I pushed myself to get back to work; we had a job to do.

Now, while all of these things were going on with me, I cannot begin to tell you what was happening with President Trump. Because despite the great conversation we had about making medicines affordable, I never heard from him again. He turned his back on the idea of lowering prescription drug costs and instead tried to roll back the Affordable Care Act (ACA) health insurance program. Nicknamed Obamacare, at that point the ACA was providing about 20 million Americans with insurance to help cover the cost of their medical expenses—doctor's appointments, medications, emergency room visits, surgery, and so on—which can be so expensive that many people choose not to go to the doctor because they don't know how they would pay the bill. Coverage that I had as a member of Congress, but that far too many Americans don't have.

That's when I realized that Trump didn't mean what he said. Instead, he'd say whatever he felt like at the time, and whoever he talked to last was who he believed. Despite what I had originally hoped for, he's *not* just a guy from the neighborhood. He's not a guy who's straight with his words, whom you can trust.

Yes, I met with Donald Trump in good faith. I thought we had a glimmer of hope, but then he lied to me. It would become one of hundreds, then thousands of lies Donald Trump would tell during the course of his presidency, not only to me but to the country and the world. In fact, after several years of his lying, *The Washington Post* calculated that Trump told about fifty lies each and every day. But during those first days of his administration, I didn't know just how many lies he would tell. None of us did. And if anyone had told us, we all would have said, "That's impossible. He's the president of the United States."

I still believe that people from different backgrounds, with different beliefs, can overcome any hurdle by working together. However, over time, I came to believe it was impossible to accomplish good things with this man. But he couldn't stop me fighting for my constituents and fighting for democracy. In fact, I was just getting started.

14

A MOMENT OF REMARKABLE POWER

I have been dealing with bullies since I was a kid. It started when I moved up from elementary to middle school. That's when I attended school with white kids for the first time. They treated me okay, especially the ones like me who wanted to learn. But of course, there were the kids, Black and white, who would bully or beat up anybody who tried to do well in school. They would applaud ignorance and scoff at excellence. They reinforced negatives and put down positives. They even ridiculed people who spoke correct English. Some kids would play dumb to fit in even though they were smart. Don't study, be tough, talk tough—these were just *some* of the things they would say.

As I grew older, I began to realize that children weren't the only people who engaged in bullying. Bullying happens everywhere—in society, movies, and television—and can involve people of any age. For example, today, a wide variety of media outlets convey harmful, negative, and insulting stereotypes of Black people. Though the mistreatment of Black people tends to be worst, many groups of people experience bullying today, including immigrants, Hispanics, Asians, the LGBTQ community, Muslims, and Jews. People of many different identities can relate to some of what Black people have experienced.

The answer is always education, education, education. It's the only thing—the one and only thing—that works. People need to better understand what bullying is and the hurt and damage that it causes. We need to know how to prevent it, how to intervene, and how to be an upstander, not a bystander who just watches what happens. Upstanders take action by telling bullies to stop, by getting others to join the united front, and by helping the victim. They take action by shifting the focus and redirecting the bully away from the victim and by telling an adult who can help.

Being an upstander is powerfully transformational.

We also have to enact laws and policies, and fight injustice. We have to educate, mobilize, advocate, and reform.

As If This Is Normal

When it exploits our nation's tender racial and ethnic divisions, bullying can have particularly dangerous and deadly consequences.

I remember two horrible, tragic events that took place: mass shootings in El Paso, Texas, and Dayton, Ohio—communities half a country away from Baltimore, yet faced with the same vulnerabilities.

A little before 11:00 a.m. on August 3, 2019, a gunman, armed with a semiautomatic AK-47, began firing shots in an El Paso Walmart parking lot. Shooting nonstop, he then entered the store, and eventually killed twenty-two people and injured twenty-four more. It was the deadliest shooting of the year. The store manager saw what was happening in the parking lot and called a "code brown," an active-shooter alert. Active-shooter alerts in schools and businesses have become routine, something that we've all come to accept, as if they are normal, like traffic signals at intersections.

But they aren't. Or they shouldn't be. There's nothing normal about this.

This mass shooting was later suspected to be a hate crime, ugly white nationalist violence aimed at Hispanic Americans. A white nationalist is someone who believes that white people are the only true Americans and that only white people should live in America. White nationalists are also white supremacists, people who believe that white people are superior to those from other racial and ethnic groups, and should dominate them. The perpetrator of this crime was a violent bully. The FBI tells us that this type of racially motivated violence by white supremacists constitutes our nation's greatest risk of domestic terrorism. Making matters worse, the shooter bought the gun from Romania, the ammunition from Russia, and by today's laws, it was all legal. Why? Why would it be legal for someone, anyone, to just order a gun from Romania and bullets from Russia?

That same day, only a few hours after the shooting in El Paso, a man in suburban Dayton, Ohio, in a nightclub area, wearing a mask and body armor, fired his weapon into a crowd, killing nine people and injuring more than twenty others. He himself was killed by police within seconds of his attack. Acquaintances described him as "an outcast" who had made threats for years and had a significant interest in violence and deep anger toward women. Investigators found evidence of his writings that exposed an interest in mass killings. Another violent bully.

Both shooters had histories that would call into question why they had access to firearms. Both had no trouble getting weapons.

Why is that okay in America? Yes, the Second Amendment to the Constitution grants citizens the right to own arms. But it doesn't give them the right to own semiautomatic, military-style weapons—and it definitely doesn't grant them the right to kill people. How long will we wring our hands and do nothing? How many times could we say the victims have our hopes and prayers? When will we do something besides hope and pray? If our nation had sensible gun control legislation, perhaps my brilliant young nephew Christopher would still be alive, even today. Maybe his parents and loved ones wouldn't have to live with broken hearts.

How long will we fail the people?

Sowing Division

Sometimes bullying takes place on Capitol Hill. It became even more common under Donald Trump, who frequently bullied people, even though he was the most powerful man in the world.

For over two years I watched President Trump attack people and institutions on Twitter—Hillary Clinton, Barack Obama, military families who had lost a loved one at war, foreign leaders, *The New York Times*, *The Washington Post*, CNN, cable news show hosts Joe Scarborough and Mika Brzezinski, the NFL, Nancy Pelosi, judges, members of his own party, entertainers . . . anyone he didn't agree with. Like a petulant child, he'd call people names if they dared to disagree with or challenge him. And this was people on all sides—Crooked Hillary, Lyin' Ted Cruz, Crazy Bernie Sanders . . . The list, and Trump's names for them, went on and on.

Elijah, at two years old, poses for his portrait.

Courtesy of Yvonne Cummings

Cummings family portrait, from left: Elijah's older brother, Robert Jr.; father, Robert Sr.; older sister, Cheretheria; mother, Ruth; and Elijah, at the time the baby of the family

Courtesy of Yvonne Cummings

Elijah and his younger brothers, Carnel and James

Courtesy of Yvonne Cummings

Elijah and his younger brother James

Courtesy of Yvonne Cummings

Elijah Cummings, look-
ing up to his older brother,
Robert Jr.

Courtesy of Yvonne Cummings

Elijah's high school photo—
Baltimore City College High School

Courtesy of Yvonne Cummings

Elijah (back row, first from left) with his youth baseball
team

Courtesy of Yvonne Cummings

Elijah with Juanita Jackson Mitchell, the attorney and civil rights pioneer who inspired him to become a lawyer

Courtesy of the Moorland-Spingarn Research Center at Howard University

Maya Rockeymoore, President Bill Clinton, First Lady Hillary Clinton, and Elijah at a White House Christmas party, 2000

White House photographer

Elijah and Maya Rockeymoore Cummingses' vow renewal
ceremony, December 2011

Kevin Brown

President Barack Obama, Vice President Joe Biden, and Elijah at the White House

White House photographer

U.S. Speaker John Boehner, Maya, and Elijah at Elijah's swearing-in ceremony for the U.S. House of Representatives, January 2015

House photographer

Elijah calms the citizens and speaks to reporters at the corner of Pennsylvania and North Avenues during the Freddie Gray unrest in Baltimore City, April 2015.

Maya Rockeymoore Cummings

Elijah and U.S. Congressman John Lewis, often called Elijah's "twin," as even the press mixed them up, in South Africa for Nelson Mandela's funeral, 2013

Congressman Bobby Scott

Maya, President Obama, and Elijah at a Bethesda fund-raiser

DCC photographer

Elijah and his mother, Ruth Cummings, with President Barack Obama at a Baltimore event

White House photographer

Speaker Nancy Pelosi, Maya, and Elijah at his swearing-in ceremony, 2019

Staff photographer

Elijah speaking to members of the Howard University choir in downtown Washington, DC

Maya Rockeymoore Cummings

Speaker Nancy Pelosi bids Elijah a solemn farewell during the lying-in-state ceremony in National Statuary Hall.

Jackie Hicks/Ashley Givens

Elijah E. Cummings was buried in Loudon Park Cemetery in Baltimore with full military honors on October 25, 2019.

Jackie Hicks/Ashley Givens

President Obama hands Maya a tissue at Elijah's home-going service at New Psalmist Baptist Church in Baltimore, October 25, 2019.

Courtesy of Jackie Hicks/Ashley Givens

A soldier presents the U.S. flag that had been draped over Elijah's coffin to his widow, Maya, at the gravesite, October 25, 2019.

Courtesy of Jackie Hicks/Ashley Givens

He made up blatant lies; as he typed his thumbs became weapons of personal destruction. In fact, rather than tweeting, he should have spent all of those hours governing, carrying out the will of the people, not engaging in his petty personal battles.

Once President Trump tried to demean some of the youngest, newest members of Congress—Ayanna Pressley (Massachusetts), Rashida Tlaib (Michigan), Ilhan Omar (Minnesota), and Alexandria Ocasio-Cortez (New York)— the so-called Squad of young, newly elected firebrands in Congress.

He went on a classic Trump tweet rampage.

Why don't they go back and help fix the totally broken and crime-infested places from which they came. Then come back and show us how it is done. These places need your help badly, you can't leave fast enough. I'm sure that Nancy Pelosi would be very happy to quickly work out free travel arrangements!

As usual, Trump didn't have his facts right. He claimed they were all from other countries, but three of the four congresswomen were born inside the United States. The president chose to stoke nationalism, xenophobia (the fear of people from foreign nations), Islamophobia, sexism, racism—basically any "ism" or "phobia" he could use—to rile up some of his supporters and divide the country. But instead of dividing the Democrats, he united us. Everyone called it what it was.

Hate.

Turning Americans against Americans.

And even though he's very powerful, the blowback from Trump's remarks was swift and hard because the Squad also have powerful voices and strong constituencies who back them. When you bully the Squad on social media, you do so at your own risk.

Standing Up to the Biggest Bully

For whatever reason, for more than two years Trump didn't go after me, even after I condemned his weak response to the "Unite the Right" white supremacists' rally in Charlottesville, Virginia, in August 2017. That's when he said there were "very fine people on both sides" of an event that included a gathering held by members of the Ku Klux Klan and neo-Nazi groups. He didn't go after me when I came down on him for pardoning Joe Arpaio, an Arizona sheriff who kept breaking the law by arresting Latinos solely because he suspected they were undocumented immigrants, even though no one had proved it. He didn't go after me when I led national hearings that exposed his business and personal character, and the breaches of law his administration had put in motion, which I'll tell you about shortly.

Sometimes I wondered why he hadn't attacked, but mostly I wondered when he would.

I knew it would come. It was just a matter of time, a matter of me doing enough to upset and challenge him, until I was his next target.

The attack happened loud and clear on July 27, 2019. Starting at 7:14 a.m., he posted this series of tweets:

Rep Elijah Cummings has been a brutal bully, shouting and screaming at the great men & women of Border Patrol about conditions at the Southern Border, when actually his Baltimore district is FAR WORSE and more dangerous. His district is considered the Worst in the USA. . . .

. . . As proven last week during a Congressional tour, the Border is clean, efficient & well run, just very crowded. Cumming District is a disgusting, rat and rodent infested mess. If he spent more time in Baltimore, maybe he could help clean up this very dangerous & filthy place.

Why is so much money sent to the Elijah Cummings district when it is considered the worst run and most dangerous anywhere in the United States. No human being would want to live there. Where is all this money going? How much is stolen? Investigate this corrupt mess immediately!

Not only was President Trump cruel, but he was, as usual, inaccurate, or just plain lying.

When Upstanders Rise

Thankfully, it took just minutes for the counterattack on Trump's hateful words. Probably not what the schoolyard bully in the White House had counted on. But the immediate response didn't come from me; it came from loud, prominent voices who rushed to my defense and the defense of the city of Baltimore and its citizens.

It came from a community of upstanders from all around the country.

> [Cummings is] . . . a champion in the Congress and the country for civil rights and economic justice —Speaker Nancy Pelosi

> Yo Trump, Hands off #ourchairman @RepCummings who is centered in American values that you will *never* understand —Congresswoman Rashida Tlaib

> Give me the rats and roaches of Baltimore any day over the lies and racism of your Washington, Mr. Trump — filmmaker John Waters

The list went on and included the other members of the Squad; Maryland's former governor Martin O'Malley; Jenna

Bush Hager, who is the daughter of former president George W. Bush; Reverend Al Sharpton; and the hosts of the morning cable talk show *Morning Joe*.

> Elijah Cummings chose to serve through challenging times . . . he comforts people who are frightened of you.
> —cable TV host Joe Scarborough

The late-night talk show hosts also weighed in. Trevor Noah, who is a person of color, said, "Yes, he's racist." Not "racially charged" or other more polite words for it. Racist.

Seth Meyers was not subtle: "another racist outburst from a racist president."

Stephen Colbert asked and answered his own question, "Previously on *Is Donald Trump Racist?* . . . Yes."

I'd be lying if I said I wasn't pleased and reassured by the outpouring of support, of fury and disgust at the president's toxic assault. No minced words. No maybes. Just honest people calling it out for what it was—racism, racism, racism.

One of the most moving defenses came from Victor Blackwell, the CNN anchor who grew up in my district and had been one of the first participants in the Elijah Cummings Youth Leadership Program. The morning of the Twitter blitz, Blackwell spoke right to the camera, to millions of viewers, from his heart, fighting back tears. It was a moment of remarkable power.

"Infested . . . we've seen the president invoke 'infestation' to criticize lawmakers before . . . Just two weeks ago, President Trump attacked four minority congresswomen: 'Why don't they go back to the totally broken and crime infested places from which they came.' Reminder, three of them were born here, all of them are American. Infested, he says. A week before his inauguration . . . [he said] 'Congressman John Lewis should spend more time on fixing and helping his district, which is in horrible shape and falling apart, not to mention crime infested.' Donald Trump has tweeted more than forty-three thousand times. He's insulted thousands of people. . . . But when he tweets about infestation, it's about Black and Brown people . . . at the height of an urgent health emergency: 'Why are we sending thousands of ill-trained soldiers into Ebola infested areas of Africa! . . .' Infested, he says. 'There's a revolution going on in California. So many sanctuary areas want out of this ridiculous, crime infested and breeding concept.' Infested, he says. The president says about Congressman Cummings's district that no human would want to live there. You know who did, Mr. President? I did, from the day I was brought home from the hospital to the day I left for college, and a lot of people I care about still do. There are challenges, no doubt. But people are proud of their community. . . . They care for their families there. They love their children, who pledge allegiance to the flag just like people who live in districts of congressmen who support you, sir. They are Americans, too."

Victor Blackwell's tears brought me to tears.

That is my city.

That is Victor's city.

And that bully was our president? Something's wrong with this picture.

A Higher Purpose Than Hate

I purposely took some time with my own retort. I gathered my thoughts and feelings. The truth is, I was hurt by what President Trump said. Deeply hurt. This is my home. These are my friends and neighbors and voters. These are human beings, flesh and blood, with feelings. With children to raise, with photos on their walls, with family dinners, with graduations to attend, with memories of the past and better hopes for the future. This man was telling them that they were less than human, that their lives were not worthwhile, that their dreams would never see the light of day. He was taking away hope. That hurt them. And when they hurt, I hurt.

But just because someone makes a bullying statement to you doesn't mean you have to respond when or how they expect. When I did reply, I would not take his bait. I would not stoop to his level. My message was my way: serious, low-key, and deeply sincere. And I purposely made my statement on Twitter, to show that it could be used for a higher purpose than hate, and to show the stark difference between our two approaches to life and our duties.

Here's what I tweeted later that day:

Mr. President, I go home to my district daily. Each morning, I wake up, and I go and fight for my neighbors. It is my constitutional duty to conduct oversight of the Executive Branch. But it is my moral duty to fight for my constituents. . . .

Every word was chosen carefully. I didn't engage in a rant, but gave him a lesson in how to serve:

"I go home to my district daily . . ."— to my home, my district, my roots, never forgetting where and what I come from—daily, every single day I possibly can from D.C. to Baltimore, to be in my district office, to be in my home, to see my constituents' faces and hear their voices—fight for my neighbors—my neighbors, my friends, sticking up for those who cannot stick up for themselves. *"It is my constitutional duty to conduct oversight . . ."*—my constitutional duty, by law, by our guiding principles. I know the Constitution, Mr. President, even if you don't. It is my duty *"to conduct oversight,"* to be the people's eyes and ears for what is going on, to watch over the executive branch because no one branch is more powerful than the others. And *". . . it is my moral duty . . ."* because I am guided by morality, whether you, Mr. President, are or not. I take my sacred duty very, very seriously.

The *Baltimore Sun*'s editorial board ran a powerful retort

headlined: "Better to have a few rats than to be one." There was no missing their message.

The *Sun*'s editorial was reprinted and reposted across the country. The headline even became a T-shirt.

It meant a lot to me to have those people come to my defense and to the defense of my city. I had been injured, wounded, knocked over—emotionally and physically. You can never picture what it is like to be assaulted, truly assaulted, by the person who sits in the most powerful office in the world. You can imagine it and try to dismiss it, saying he's just a schoolyard tough guy, using his thumbs on Twitter like fists. But the reality, the harsh cold onslaught, is just pure pain.

I recall talking to someone about it at the time.

"This hurts. It hurts. It brings me pain. So much I could be dead," I blurted out.

"What do you mean dead? Politically dead? No way," the person replied.

"No! I'm talking about dead. Not alive. D-E-A-D, dead."

I didn't mean some kind of expression. I meant a fact. It could kill me.

You see, ever since my surgery for aortic stenosis, I could feel the storm unfolding within my body. Yet I worked early; I worked late; I drafted and reviewed legislation; I returned emails in the middle of the night; I conferred with colleagues at all hours. But while once I walked around Capitol Hill, I now needed a cane and a walker to move in my office in the Rayburn House Office Building. I used a motorized scooter to go from Rayburn to the U.S. Capitol. I did this without complaint. There's no such word as can't.

But there's no way to know where the line is between body and soul, between head and heart—and I could feel President Trump's attack to my core.

Did it make me weaker physically?

No doubt.

Did the support of others make me stronger in my resolve?

No doubt.

On August 3, I spoke at the opening of a park in Baltimore, a green space, a playground—no rats, no rodents, just happy children and parents—a stark contrast to the way the president characterized my home.

I told the crowd that I did not have time or patience or tolerance for people who trash my city, but I always have time for our children.

"When I hear criticism by anybody about my city, I think the thing that bothers me most is that we have a situation where there are folks who are stepping on the foot, on the hope of our children. I don't know what I would have done if I'd had people in high places when I was a little boy telling me what I couldn't do. Instead, I had people telling me what I could do."

Then I told the media folks who were there that I'd like

President Trump to visit Baltimore, to see the real Baltimore, but of course, I doubted he would ever accept that invitation.

Have you ever experienced a time when a bully targeted you? Did the thought of standing up to them seem overwhelming? How did you approach the situation? Did an upstander help you? If so, how? If not, how would you have liked an upstander to protect you?

I was fortunate enough to receive a lot of support after President Trump bullied me. Is there someone you know who you can tell about what may have hurt you in the past? Consider confiding in your parents or guardian, a relative, a teacher, a coach, a youth leader, or a trusted friend.

Looking beyond yourself, are there others—in your class, on your sports team, in your community—who could use the same kind of support that I got after I was bullied? Who might you consider being an upstander for? Who needs the same type of support that my friends and coworkers gave me?

15

HEARING THE HUE AND CRY

Earlier in the summer of 2019, before the president's assault, I had been invited to speak at the National Press Club, a century-old organization for professional journalists. My speech was scheduled to take place on August 7, which turned out to be less than two days after Donald Trump had bullied me, declaring war on me and my home.

I planned to take a stand about what I thought the president should be doing rather than wasting precious time bullying me and the city I love. I planned to defend Baltimore. I wanted to talk about the great work so many people are doing there. But I also intended to discuss prescription drug prices, the importance of decency and respect in politics, and some of the work we had been doing on the Oversight Committee. I urged Congress to return from recess to address gun violence, and told them that my mother, on her deathbed, told me we must protect the vote.

Normally, a late-summer speech at the National Press Club would have drawn a crowd of unexceptional size and modest media coverage—barely enough to fill a small space. But now that President Trump had attacked me and my city, suddenly there was lots of interest. After being restrained and quiet for so many days, the time had come for me to make a powerful public statement, to stand up to the bully in front of the cameras. To use my voice and demonstrate my power, my love of my home, of my family. Today, I do my best to use my voice to protect against threats, abuse, or ambush by anyone. Attack my city, you attack me. But I want you to know that I wasn't always like this.

Moments That Shaped Me

Moments occur when I am amazed to see my growth as a person, as an elected official, as a servant of the people. I remember well when I was still a boy born Elijah who was embarrassed of his name. I still have in my memory how frightened I felt when we walked through the neighborhood of angry white adults so we could swim in the public pool.

And I can even recall, as if it was yesterday, a time during my adulthood when I would attend a press conference with other members of Congress and think to myself, *What do I have to say? What do I have to offer that matters? The others seem to all know what to do. What am I doing here?*

During my earlier days in Congress, I would freeze up and let others speak—they seemed so eloquent. When the press conference was finally over, I'd just go home. Then I would tell Maya about it, how I froze, and she'd remind me that my thoughts and opinions were unique; they were mine, from my heart, from my constituents, my streets, and my life.

"Tell them. Tell them what you know, what you've seen, what you feel," my wife, Maya, would encourage.

So over the years I pushed myself. I'd step forward and open my mouth, and I'd will the words to come out. You might say, I'd fake it until it was real. And, sure enough, I discovered I did have something to say. I did have the experiences and the ideas that people wanted to hear.

My reluctance to speak began to disappear.

Pretty soon other people were quoting me. They'd say, "As Elijah Cummings said . . ."

I discovered how to use my ability to speak and use words to convey powerful ideas that can reach people and open their minds to different viewpoints.

It took me a long time to learn to use my voice, but once

I learned how, it was formidable. So now I will not be silent when the president or his foot soldiers attempt to intimidate me or others, to suppress people's vote, restrict it, or find a way to reinvent Jim Crow laws. Certain days require me to speak truth in the face of doubters and enemies, in the glare of hot lights and cameras, under the threats of a president, or when someone has to take the lead. On these occasions, I look back to the experiences, the moments that shaped me more than any others in my life.

My parents prepared me.

My faith prepared me.

But one formative, lasting, indelible event forged my character and shaped me into who I have become, but I didn't even know it was strengthening me in this way. I believe in my heart of hearts, in my soul, that taking those trips to integrate the swimming pool as a young child made me stronger. Though they took place long ago, they prepared me for my life, and for moments in the spotlight when I must stand up for what's right.

There was an obvious hurdle in front of all of us as we marched to the pool. We faced harsh backlash for doing what we knew was fair, for demanding our equality. But was the payoff worth it? A hundred percent yes. And if I hadn't learned these things then, I may not have been able to be the upstander I am now, when I want to take people not just to common ground, but to higher ground. That is how this difficult moment shaped me. Now, the time had come for me to use my voice and speak the truth.

An Unexpected Turn

So much buzz was building about my speech at the National Press Club that they had to move us to a much bigger room. I was both confident and prepared. After all these years, I had a lot to say. And I was determined to say it. I would use my voice.

But a couple of days before my speech, my life took a sudden and unexpected turn that almost caused me not to get my chance.

After countless months of working so hard—and being bullied by the most powerful man in the world—I'd become weaker than I'd been in years. Then in late July, I nearly collapsed.

My doctor sent me right to Johns Hopkins, where I was told I had pneumonia. However, the underlying suspicion was that the cancer I'd been fighting off and on for twenty years had come back.

I was still in a hospital bed the morning of my speech, on IV fluids and meds, barely able to move.

"I'm going to give that speech if I have to crawl," I said to Maya. I had a sense that my fate was written and my time limited, but my mind was made up: I would make this speech.

I did not crawl, but I didn't run, either. My medical team

understood what I had to do. They allowed me to leave Baltimore to go to Washington with medical care nearby. They said I could give my speech, answer people's questions, and get back to the hospital in four hours, not a minute longer.

Better Than This

On the morning of the event, my car arrived at the Press Club, I was wheeled into the room, and then assisted to my seat on the dais. The place was packed: cameras, microphones, reporters, national anchors, and investigative reporters.

When my time to speak came, I had to be helped to my feet and a stool was placed near the podium just in case I had to sit. After that, I didn't need any more help. I had already gone through the ritual I follow before every speech. I rehearse with God. I look out at the audience, I soak them in, I get a "feel" for the place and time, the moment. I was ready. I had always treated every speech as if it was my last. Today that was truer than any before. This speech, this day, was my destiny.

I stood quietly and looked out at the faces. I waited. I breathed. And then I spoke.

"God has called me to this moment. I did not ask for it."

Even though I was in pain—body and spirit—it fueled my passion, my mission. Yes, I had a true purpose that day. I had summoned my strength for a reason. I was there to use my voice to deliver a message to the messengers—the media—to carry back to their readers, listeners, followers, bloggers, and posters. I wanted them to hear the hue and cry of our people against the injustices, the cruelty, the divisiveness that were all too fast becoming commonplace, almost normal.

I wanted the messengers to hear the message and shout it out to everyone and say, "No! We will not let it happen! No! We're better than this. We're so much better than this."

I recounted the horrors of the gun violence of El Paso and Dayton and our failure as a government to do anything about it, anything but offer prayers and inadequate sorrow. I condemned the fact that we were letting people die because they couldn't afford the medicines that could keep them alive, and our failure to do anything about it.

I relived the attacks the president had levied against me and my city and so many others, attacks we all know are ugly, and evil and immoral . . . and our failure to do anything about them. I railed, loud and full-throated, against ignoring the Constitution, assailing our right to vote, threatening our democracy, and our failure to do anything about it.

But we—the people and the free press—can do something about it.

We are not powerless.

I used my voice to remind the messengers of their duty to report and inform, over and over, relentlessly. And how the country needs it now more than ever. I invoked Martin Luther King's words, "our silence becomes our betrayal." I told them not to be silent. I told them to speak up. I said I know they were told to turn off their cell phones when they came in, but I said no, they should turn them on, then and there. They should text and email and tweet to get the messages out—to legislators, to readers, to preachers, to everyone they could.

"This is a fight for the soul of our democracy," I said loud and clear. My words hit home. I knew it by the repeated interruptions of applause and shout-outs. They clapped, and they stood, and they hollered even more. I told them how much I appreciated their support.

I was humbled.

And tired. So tired.

But I wasn't quite done.

I stayed until I had answered every question I possibly could. I had stayed to the limit of my hospital pass, perhaps longer. It was time to keep my promise and make my way back to Johns Hopkins.

When I returned to the hospital, I was spent. I crawled back into my bed and lay there for hours and days, recovering from that short journey. But it was worth enduring the pain to communicate my passion. I was rewarded with accolades over the next few days. To each one, I responded the same: "Thank you for your words. But more than your words, I need your help."

Each day I thought I'd be stronger and go home, or go

back to the Hill "tomorrow." Tomorrow stretched into the day after. And the day after. I never stopped working. I worked from my hospital bed. I had meetings in my room. I made conference calls and signed subpoenas. I attended the Democratic caucus sessions by phone. Then, blessedly, Congress went on recess. And it's a good thing. Because I would need some serious rest for what was up ahead.

16

THE GREATEST CHECK

I hadn't known that I would end up in Congress; however, my entire life had prepared me to be a congressional representative. I'd spent a lifetime striving to help others, from growing up in South Baltimore and rising from those streets to the U.S. Congress. I'm a Democrat—but more than a party, I believe in people, in freedom, in opportunity, in country, and in making sure we have a democracy to leave our children. I've spent most of my adult life serving the public because I believe that is why I was put on this earth. That may sound lofty but it's what I feel to my very core.

Along the way, from time to time, my father would retell the story about how his father died. The story of my grandfather never left him, and it pushed him to be sure his own family received proper health care, but as I mentioned before, even that was a struggle, as we didn't always have access and often had to resort to home remedies to deal with things like tooth pain. During my adulthood, I, too, have fought so that the American public could obtain affordable health care and medicine. The Congressional Black Caucus, which I once led, also thought health care was an important issue.

Not in Our Democracy

Now, I and the rest of the nation were left to live in and run a nation led by Donald Trump. President Trump governed, if we can call it that, with a total disregard for, or ignorance of, the Constitution, of our system of governing, and of democracy.

He often used the term "fake news" to describe the press anytime they reported on things that made him look bad. But the truth was, they were just trying to keep our citizens aware of what was going on. Though the press is not a formal part of the government, it helps to prevent misdeeds by government officials. It acts in addition to the checks and balances by the executive, legislative, and judicial branches. The media called Trump out on his lies and unconscionable behavior. He didn't like what was being said about him, so he tried to discredit it.

Normally, working for the president of the United States is the honor of a lifetime. But more people left the Trump administration than any other in history—fired, pushed out, or they resigned because they were fed up with working for him. They include generals, press secretaries, security advisors, lawyers, and heads of major departments of the U.S. government.

Trump also abandoned our nation's longtime allies—Mexico, Australia, even Canada and NATO. And he cozied up to some of the world's biggest tyrants—Vladimir Putin in Russia, Kim Jong-un of North Korea, and Recep Tayyip Erdogan of Turkey.

He threatened Republican politicians who questioned him, warning that he would help their rivals challenge and defeat them during primary elections. He gave a low-key approval to white supremacists after the Unite the Right rally. That was the same event where one of his white nationalist followers intentionally rammed a car into a crowd of counterprotesters, killing an innocent young woman, Heather Heyer, and seriously injuring many others.

Trump had encouraged and/or pushed world leaders to stay at Trump hotels around the world, enriching himself from the presidency, a direct violation of the Constitution's emoluments clause. What the emoluments clause means, in plain English, is that no one holding federal office can receive a gift, payment, or anything of value from a foreign state or a foreign ruler or representative. For example, the president of the United States can't or shouldn't accept money or payment, directly or through a company he owns, from a government official—president, prime minister, king, queen, emissary, dignitary, ambassador, etc. In other words, those officials shouldn't be staying, eating, or playing golf at one of the president's hotels, resorts, condos, or whatever.

But as of June 2019, NBC said at least twenty-two foreign governments had spent money at properties owned by President Trump's business, the Trump Organization, directly violating the emoluments clause.

Wink-winking at white supremacist groups? Cozying up to dangerous world leaders? Blatant disregard for constitutional rules? We had never seen a leader act like this in our lifetimes. At least not in a democracy, and certainly not in our democracy.

From Rumble to Roar

I sensed the next few months were going to be different in Congress—both for the country and for me personally. It was maybe the most critical time I'd faced in my life. A word that had been whispered and threatened almost since the day Donald Trump announced his run for president became real: impeachment.

Impeachment is the legal process the founding fathers

created for Congress to follow to charge a government official with "treason, bribery, or other high crimes and misdemeanors." The meanings of treason and bribery are clear. The founding fathers left it to Congress to interpret "high crimes and misdemeanors," which basically means a major crime, political offense, or other seriously improper behavior.

Impeachment is the greatest check that the legislative branch can exert on the executive branch to protect our nation from the seemingly limitless power that the British monarchy once had. But what's a "high crime"? Not everyone agrees. The Constitution entrusted the House of Representatives with making the charges and the Senate with holding the trial. One of the possible penalties of impeachment is removal from office.

Because of all his many infractions, people had been hoping for a possible impeachment. Only one month into his new presidency, a political action group was formed to do just that. This took place even though Republicans, members of the president's party, controlled both houses of Congress. In other words, neither the House nor Senate would cooperate with any inquiry into impeachment. But the growing list of violations caused the issue to gather momentum. One of the earliest voices, Congressman Al Green of Texas, spoke out in favor of Trump's possible impeachment publicly. In private, however, plenty of the Democratic leaders agreed, but most, like myself, believed we should proceed carefully and cautiously. Rather than coming after him right away, we decided to allow the evidence to build over time.

In May 2017, the Justice Department had assigned Robert Mueller—a former FBI director who served during the George W. Bush and Barack Obama administrations—to investigate whether Russia had interfered in the 2016 election by illegally cooperating with the Trump campaign to help him win. In June, James Comey, the former FBI director under both President Obama and President Trump, testified under oath in front of Congress, saying that the president had pressured him to be loyal to Trump rather than loyal to the country. This went directly against the oath Comey took upon joining the FBI, and so Comey didn't give the president the answer he wanted. Shortly after that, Trump fired him.

Comey's firing was enough to cause Congressman Brad Sherman of California to join Congressman Green in drafting articles of impeachment, which kickstarted the process of leveling impeachment charges against the president. These articles accused President Trump of obstruction of justice during Mueller's investigation of whether Russia had interfered with the election.

That August, after the Unite the Right rally where Trump subtly supported white supremacists, Congressman Steve Cohen of Tennessee joined the movement to impeach him. Cohen stated that Trump had "failed the presidential test of moral leadership."

On December 6, 2017, Congressman Al Green introduced

a resolution, or legislation, to impeach the president. It accused Trump of "Associating the Presidency with White Nationalism, Neo-Nazism and Hatred" and "Inciting Hatred and Hostility." He introduced another resolution on January 19, 2018.

Up to this point, as the minority party in Congress, most of the Democrats in leadership, myself included, were against taking formal action on impeachment. Our strategy was to keep gathering evidence. But the public was moving toward the possibility of impeachment slowly and steadily, and Trump's popularity in his own party was dropping significantly. What had been a rumble became a roar.

As leaders, we always considered the math—how many people would we need to impeach him and how many to convict? The House can impeach a president if a majority agree to do so, but to convict, we'd need two-thirds of the Senate to sign on. With the Republicans in control of the House, the resolution was defeated.

The Three Monkeys

In the meantime, we had business to conduct.

In our disastrous predicament with the Trump administration and all the brick walls we'd encountered, it would have been easy to give up, to say, "I can't find a solution." It would have been easy to believe that this geometry problem can't be solved.

I wasn't willing to give up that easily. I'd heard many of my congressional colleagues, both Republicans and Democrats, say that they planned to leave Congress soon, or would not even try to run again, because they couldn't get anything meaningful done, they couldn't get through to the White House, or the president himself, to do what needed to be done for their constituents.

I understand. I empathize. But I don't agree with throwing in the towel.

Sure, I get frustrated, angry, even outraged over things like our failure to pass legislation on important problems like the opioid crisis, the Affordable Care Act, voting rights, immigration, you name it. Both sides agree we need to address these issues. But we must not give up. We must find solutions.

We must learn from our errors and from each other. The stakes are very high, and the American people deserve nothing less. We have to go back to our homework until we get it right.

Just like I learned in geometry.

Aha!

But the Republican majority didn't want to take a hard look at what was going on, or where we'd gone so wrong, and they sure didn't want to fix it. They behaved like the three monkeys—hear no evil, see no evil, speak no evil. Just pretend everything is okay. Just worry about keeping your seat in Congress.

In addition to flouting all the rules, the Trump administration had been obstructing Congress in an attempt to prevent us from doing our job. Our challenge was to get around, over, and through that obstruction.

And it turns out, we weren't the only people getting angry at it. More and more of the American public wanted to remove President Trump and his administration from power so the leadership and the nation would be fairer.

The Blue Wave

Fortunately, no matter how much we hate or love the winning candidates, we still hold elections. And it's during these election cycles that, if America isn't happy with existing candidates, we can cast our vote to turn the tides. The presidential cycle is every four years. But in Congress, it's every six years for senators, and every two years for representatives.

Halfway through the Trump administration, people were mad. At the two-year mark of every president's four-year term, the nation holds what are called midterm elections. The midterms provide feedback on how the public believes the president and congressional leadership are doing and whether they need the public to implement more checks and balances. The Democrats thought we might win the House back. But we were realistic in assuming the Senate would still be controlled by the Republicans.

During the midterm campaigns, impeachment was a big

issue, on both sides. In liberal and swing districts where the issue appealed to Democrats and independents, the Democratic candidates raised it often. In more conservative districts, Republican candidates used it as a rallying cry to defend the president. Politically, areas that tend to be more liberal, or Democratic, are often called "blue." Those that lean conservative, or Republican, are referred to as "red." And swing districts are usually known as "purple," where there's a political mix of the two and likely lots of independent voters, who might swing from party to party.

It's important to know this because during the 2016 presidential election, some regions that had historically been blue had gone red for Trump. But now, at the halfway point, Trump's day-to-day conduct—constantly nasty, constantly threatening, constantly shameful—was making some of his supporters regret voting him in.

We thought he was going to drain the swamp, people would say. *But now the swamp is deeper and dirtier than ever.*

People were mad and they showed it at the polls. The number of voters who turned out for the 2018 midterm elections was the highest in over a hundred years. In fact, voter turnout in non-presidential years had been going steadily down, until 2018. The last time we had a strong showing at the polls was at the height of the Vietnam War and protests, when millions of people were angry about the government's commitment to the war and all that went with it—the draft, the social unrest, and deaths of our soldiers in a battle between two sides most of us didn't understand.

That November, the Democrats won back the House from the Republicans in what we call a blue wave—a dramatic upswell in the public's support of Democrats. Thankfully, two years earlier my constituents reelected me to the House with more than 75 percent of the vote, so, feeling somewhat safe, I set out to help every Democrat I possibly could—in swing districts, inner cities, rural farmlands, anywhere we could win a seat.

This wave gave us Democrats the feedback that the public wanted us to be more aggressive on impeachment. The record voter turnout was largely a reaction and backlash to the way Trump and his one-sided Congress had governed for his first two years.

The November 2018 election cycle wasn't only a time in which more minorities, people of color, and LGBTQ people won elections. More than anything, it was the year of women. Suddenly after years of there being hardly any women in Congress, in the House there were now 102 (89 Democrats, 13 Republicans), with 31 of those females being first-timers, including the first Democratic Latina governor and two Native Americans, one of whom is the first openly LGBTQ Native American woman member of Congress. The newcomers also included the first two Muslim women in Congress, the first Black woman elected from Massachusetts, and the youngest woman ever elected to Congress, at twenty-nine years old.

The Democratic candidates homed in like lasers on issues that had energized so many voters to turn out, including the Republicans' threat to health care overall, their possible participation in Russian interference in the 2016 election, their furthering of income inequality and tax cuts for the wealthy, immigration cruelty, and racial division. These new congresswomen and -men represented the desire of voters to halt all of that, to try to reverse the damage, and to hopefully start anew.

17

POWER AND RESPONSIBILITY

"You teach people how to treat you." My mother's words still ring true, no matter my age.

Teaching people how to treat you—it's very important.

As I have developed relationships and friendships in the United States Congress, I've thought back to my mother's words many times. Democracy literally means "a government run by the people." People don't always agree. But to get anywhere, especially in the polarizing arena of politics, we have to find common ground, something to build trust and respect on. You also have to teach people that you have boundaries, bottom lines, things you will not do, behaviors you won't put up with, places you will not go. As in a democracy, having our own checks and balances teaches our friends, as well as our leaders, what we will and will not accept.

Act Better Than the Other Person

In addition to helping me hold the high moral ground in my reply to the bullying of Donald Trump, my mother's lesson helped me keep my cool during a challenging experience with a fellow congressman, one that could be chalked up to political disagreement, but felt more like a personal offense. Some might even go as far as to call it abuse.

During the Obama administration, Republican congressman Darrell Issa was the chair of the House Committee on Oversight and Reform. The committee was in the midst of hearings. We had a witness on the stand and the chairman and other members had asked a lot of questions and made their statements. I had one more statement to make. But Congressman Issa decided we had all said and learned enough. He would not allow me to speak, which would have been disrespectful to any member of Congress, but even more so to me as a ranking member. What's even worse is that he stood up, said, "We're adjourned," and quickly shut down the mics and abruptly ended the hearing.

Then he did something that sent a cold chill through the

room. He gave a slash-across-the-neck motion—some called it a lynching gesture. I tried to speak even without a microphone, to say that this is not the way any member of Congress should be treated, not the way the government should work, or the way we should conduct a democracy. But I couldn't be heard.

That was hardly the end of it.

Democrats and some Republicans immediately reacted to Issa's gesture, calling it an ugly reminder of ugly history—the Ku Klux Klan, self-styled justice, racism, killing people by hanging them from trees. A motion was proposed on the floor to condemn him for that act.

I did not join that fray. I let the others do it.

But ultimately the motion was not passed.

Of course, the media jumped on it. Issa and the slash, along with all the hate and bigotry it conjured up, were on every nightly news report.

I did not add to the fire.

I only addressed the need for everyone to be heard in the democratic process. Then the Congressional Black Caucus called for Issa's removal as chairman of the committee.

Not too much later, I got a call directly from Darrell Issa. He apologized to me personally. Then he told the press, "As chairman, I should have been more sensitive to the mood of what was going on, and I take responsibility."

But what happened up to that point was only half of my

mother's lesson. The other half came shortly after.

There is a tradition in Congress that the portrait of each chairperson is hung in a formal ceremony. All members of the committee are invited to attend. It was time for Darrell Issa's portrait to be placed. But the pain of the slashing gesture was still fresh. Should I attend? Should I refuse?

A day or so before the ceremony was to occur, I spoke to my then-eighty-five-year-old mother. I told her I wasn't sure what to do.

"Elijah, absolutely you should go," she told me. "This man made you famous."

Not only was she telling me that you teach people how to treat you, she was also showing me exactly how to do it. You must act better than the other person.

I took her advice. I went, I even spoke, and in my speech, I quoted my mother telling me to go, telling me that Darrell Issa, in his way, had made me more prominent.

From that day on, Darrell Issa treated me with the utmost respect. I had taught him that I would not put up with poor treatment—and that even when he'd behaved disrespectfully toward me, I would still show him respect.

As I've already told you, my most sacred relationship is with God, and he teaches us that forgiveness and understanding are the important things we can do as people. So I demonstrated forgiveness toward Darrell Issa. Afterward, I would even say we became friends. We were almost always on opposite sides of issues, but worked as equals in search of answers.

I've called upon my mother's lesson over and over through my career and my life. Not just with Darrell Issa, but with others across the aisle. Despite our differences, we taught each other how to treat each other. How can I do that? Why do I do it? My parents, and the church, taught me not to demonize people, even if they had committed a bad deed, but rather to allow for redemption. Sometimes that is very hard to do, to forgive or allow for the possibility of forgiveness, but I try.

I remind myself that we are all flawed, and I hope that when the time comes when I'm in the wrong, other folks will do the same for me.

A few years ago, Maya and I heard Bryan Stevenson, founder of the Equal Justice Initiative—an organization whose mission includes fighting for prisoners on death row— speak in Washington, D.C.

Stevenson's words stayed with me.

"Each of us is better than the worst thing we have done," he said.

I believe that. I try very hard to practice that belief.

And I do something else. Something that is sometimes good, sometimes not so good. I compartmentalize, a defense mechanism that requires that you suppress your emotions and feelings. Compartmentalizing helps me keep my emotions in the right place. I try to separate who someone is as a person from their actions and deeds. If their actions or deeds are wrong, I do my best to not hold them in that negative light forever, but instead have a chance to repent. That's what I did with Darrell Issa. And it has helped me extend grace to people, move on from their wrongdoings, and take steps forward toward a more peaceful future.

And it didn't take long for a turnabout to come around.

Far from My Humble Beginnings

On January 4, 2019, California congresswoman Nancy Pelosi became the Speaker of the House, the leader of the House of Representatives. It's the third-highest-ranking position in all of the U.S. government. She invited me to be chair of the House Committee on Oversight and Reform, to lead one of the most powerful committees in the government—the committee Darrell Issa was chairing when he cut me off.

"I am humbled and honored to be the next chairman of the primary investigative body of Congress," I uttered as I was sworn in on the first day of the 116th Congress, the twenty-third year I'd served.

All these many years and many unlikely events later, life had brought me a long way from my humble beginnings. I had progressed from being the son of sharecroppers, a boy who struggled in school, to neighborhood advocate, to a member of the Maryland state legislature, to U.S. congressman, to one of the nation's most powerful lawyers. I'd reached the top of a profession that a school counselor had once told me was too high for me to aspire toward.

Oversight and Reform can investigate anything related to federal employees—how much people are paid, their retirement programs, how departments purchase supplies, how our population gets counted, the delivery of mail—you name it. The chair of that committee is one of only a few leaders with the power to order a member of government to appear without even asking its members if they agree. It's a tremendously powerful position. Now that we had the majority in the House, we Democrats would have real clout. But to me and others in leadership, that was all the more reason to use it wisely. I believe it's the chair's job to conduct him- or herself with a conscience. That's what the committee essentially is—the government's conscience. The chair should use the authority of a congressional committee as a responsibility and not a weapon. With power comes great responsibility.

When it was time to add new members to the committee, I told Nancy to give me newly elected representatives. There are twenty-two members on the committee, plus myself. Nancy gave me five who are in their first terms, several who are members of the Squad—Alexandria Ocasio-Cortez, Ayanna Pressley, and Rashida Tlaib. Three more were only in their second year. That's a lot of young folks. But I love the enthusiasm and energy of young members. I love the opportunity to mentor, and I love to learn from them as much as I teach them. A good mentor should learn from their mentees, and mentees should always look for things they can teach their mentor.

Now we were ready to carry out the stated job of the committee. We had to do the first part of our work—oversee, look carefully, study, uncover—before we could do the next part—repair, restore, even resuscitate our damaged democracy. I knew that we had two years, maybe more if the Democrats maintained our majority come the next election. But we couldn't count on that. When I took over, oversight had been neglected, or rather avoided thus far during the Trump administration. With no oversight, there was no reform, so we immediately dug in.

To me there were two sets of concerns: 1) the use and abuse of power by the Trump administration. After twenty-four months of the Trump presidency, a staggering mass of allegations warranted investigation—cooperation with foreign governments, interfering and tampering with the election process, business deals that broke the rules for what a president can and cannot do, money paid to silence people from telling the truth, conflicts of interest, an attempt to ban Muslims from entering the country, attacks on the FBI's reputation, veiled and overt personal threats, and guilty people who Trump was implying he'd pardon. But too much remained to be done before we could start on that process, so we chose to begin with 2) defending our democracy. Defending democracy included examining prescription drug prices, ensuring voting rights, addressing issues like the opioid crisis, affordable health care, immigration, and children's welfare. So we rolled up our sleeves.

The Trump White House would do everything possible to block us at every turn. Thus far, they had demonstrated a total disdain and disrespect for the Constitution and the balance of power the founding fathers established. But there is an old adage that says, "The wheels of justice turn slowly but grind exceedingly fine." I might add "especially in a democracy." And "especially in a government built on checks and balances, on the separation of powers."

This is the foundation of civics that young people are taught in school and that everyone who undertakes a career in public service also understands.

Almost everyone.

The forty-fifth president of the United States did not comprehend civics, and when he was forced to deal with it, he didn't like it.

Shocking and Frightening

On January 10, 2019, the Oversight Committee launched what would amount to the most in-depth investigation into the pharmaceutical industry's pricing practices that had ever occurred to that point. The pharmaceutical industry consists of a group of businesses that do scientific research so they can make medicines to treat people's health challenges and diseases. You or someone you know might take medicine for, say, anxiety, attention deficit disorder, asthma, cancer, depression, diabetes, high blood pressure, and so on—those are all considered pharmaceutical medications.

Our committee sent written requests to twelve leading pharmaceutical companies requesting information. Much of what we asked about involved their prices and power.

We had a lot of information about drug costs and drug profits before the investigations began. This information was shocking, sometimes frightening.

Here's an example. Between 2011 and 2015, the price of most prescription drugs doubled. In 2018, drug costs increased again. The companies are pricing drugs so high that many people can no longer afford them. One survey showed that 20 percent, or one out of every five people, did not fill a prescription because it cost too much! Think about that when you walk down the street. Count the next five people and realize the fifth one cannot afford his or her medicine.

We knew a lot going into the hearings. But we knew there was a lot we didn't know. So we asked the leaders in the industry: Tell us how you run your business. Just tell us how it works—why you charge what you charge. No surprise, they didn't want us, or anyone, looking into their practices. But if the House Committee on Oversight and Reform makes a formal request, what could they do?

One Woman, Two Daughters

The true impact and tragedy of the crisis came to life when Antoinette Worsham, mother of two daughters, both type 1 diabetics, told us her story. Her older daughter, Antavia, was diagnosed at the age of sixteen but only lived to twenty-two, solely because insulin is so expensive that she self-rationed. That's a nice way of saying she cut her doses in half or less in the hope she could survive, even weaker and more at risk, by stretching the medicine out.

The doctor didn't tell her to ration her insulin. She did it because she had no choice. It was all she could afford. It's like diluting soup until it's nothing but water and no nutrition. It doesn't work, at least not for long. When type 1 diabetics ration insulin, in time it can cause them to go into a coma.

Eventually you die.

And she did . . . because she couldn't get the drug that could keep her alive. No other reason.

I wanted the committee and the country to hear that, to hear a mother talk about losing her daughter. I wanted people to feel what it would be like to lose a child for a reason that could have been prevented. I hoped maybe even the president could feel that.

But even after sharing Antavia's tragic story with the committee, Antoinette wasn't finished. She told us about her younger daughter, Antanique, who was diagnosed with the same disease when she was twelve, and was now eighteen and a freshman in college.

"I fear the same thing will happen to Antanique when she turns twenty-one," Antoinette said to us.

I wanted everyone in that room to feel that fear. Imagine losing a child only to lose another the very same way. A way that is preventable. A way that we could stop with the stroke of a pen. Even the harshest cynics on the committee were silent and stunned as she spoke.

"How do pharmaceutical companies think college students are supposed to be able to pay for high drug costs on top of high tuition, room and board?" she asked. "How is allowing pharmaceuticals to price-gouge making America great again?"

This mother calling out the pharmaceutical companies' excessive focus on profits was more compelling than any testimony from a doctor or nurse or research scientist. And instead of waiting on the Trump administration to change, Antoinette Worsham decided to do something herself. She founded T1Diabetes Journey Inc. in honor of her older daughter, Antavia, to give financial help to people with diabetes.

One woman.

Alone.

"We need them to fight for affordable health care for all," she pleaded. "Not just for those living below or just above poverty."

But the government was ignoring the issue. She even

laid out the math: a student fresh out of college could make around \$40,000 or \$3,333 a month. If you subtract \$800 for rent, \$300 for a car, \$170 for auto insurance, \$500 for food, \$200 for health insurance, another \$200 for utilities and phone, \$500 to pay back student loans, \$150 miscellaneous, and \$1,000 for insulin—subtract those expenses and the diabetic comes up almost \$500 short. Every month. That's six thousand dollars of debt a year. Just to stay alive. She had our attention and literally begged for our help: "I am crying out and asking for you to review the pharmaceutical drug gouging and make health care affordable for all."

I saw tears in the eyes of my colleagues. I saw sympathy and empathy. I had hope. But we did not see any action. In fact, we saw the opposite. We saw obstruction.

As we prepared for the next step in the hearings and investigations, which was to request that the drug companies give us documents and testify in front of us, Republican members of the committee openly urged the companies and their executives *not* to comply with our requests. Two of the committee's Republican leaders, Jim Jordan and Mark Meadows, sent a letter to the pharmaceutical companies, claiming that we were out to destroy their firms. It was a blatant scare tactic—a false, bizarre conspiracy theory—which would prevent us from helping people afford their medicines.

I was outraged and appalled.

But I would not be bullied.

For too many people, this is a life-or-death issue. Being able to afford medicine keeps people alive. And that's *all* people, no matter which side of the aisle you're on. Democrats, Republicans, young, old, Black, white, Brown, straight, LGBTQ. Everyone. The cost of prescription drugs affects every single person in the country. Americans pay more for our medicines than people in any other Western nation. We pay too much for the privilege to live. It should be a right.

It was the exact same issue I raised to Trump on our first meeting after he took office. I told him that taking action to lower costs was something he could do for all people, not just his supporters. It was something that would benefit everyone.

Almost everyone. The pharmaceutical companies are the only group in the United States that opposes more reasonable pricing.

Just like my first meeting with Trump, the hearings provided a fleeting hope. The Republicans said whatever seemed like the right thing to say at the time. But it was short-lived. The drug companies and their lobbyists did their best to blunt our efforts. *Poof*, the hope for change was gone, or, at least, put on hold.

How do we tell Antoinette Worsham to hold? She's already lost one daughter and may lose another.

We hit a roadblock. But this was not the end of our journey, just a detour. I could still hear my father telling me the story of his father, the South Carolina preacher who died because two doctors said he was too poor, and maybe too Black, to matter, to get the care and medicine that might have saved him. I could see the faces of the folks in my neighborhood, and across the country, who have to decide between food on the table and prescriptions. No, I was not giving up. I was determined to continue the battle for health care, starting with lowering drug costs. This was the start, not the finish.

Unspeakable Methods

The committee also began to examine the many issues raised by the Trump administration's approach to immigration. Our nation is better than so many of the policies, statements, and behaviors that have come from the Trump White House, particularly its policies related to our southwestern border.

America is a nation of immigrants. Other than the indigenous Native American population and the African Americans whose ancestors were brought here enslaved, virtually everyone else chose to migrate here or is a descendant of those immigrants. The Statue of Liberty greets newcomers to our nation with these glorious words: "Give me your tired, your poor, your huddled masses yearning to breathe free. . . ."

But some people only want highly educated immigrants who come from wealthy nations, particularly European countries. So even though people who want to migrate to the United States may be running from terror or injustice, or seeking refuge from famine or flood, or may have wonderful gifts and humanity to share with our nation—just as their critics' ancestors once did—some people don't want us to let them in or allow them to earn the ability to one day become citizens.

Over the past five years, many people from Central America have walked hundreds of miles toward nations like Panama, Mexico, and the United States hoping to be offered asylum, the political protection that many nations offer to refugees. Refugees are people who have left their nation due to war, political persecution, or a national disaster, such as an earthquake, hurricane, or famine. Central American refugees are usually fleeing gangs, violence, political persecution, poverty, hate crimes against LGBTQ people, and other difficulties. Refugees are desperate.

When they reached our nation's southwestern border and attempted to follow the legal process to seek asylum, the Trump administration implemented unspeakable methods in an effort to keep these refugees out. Among the most wicked policies, the administration literally split families apart at the border. So the Oversight Committee launched an investigation into what, back then, were the rumors and reports we had been receiving about it.

Damning Evidence

If ever there was a job for young, outspoken, idealistic

crusaders—aka the Squad—this was it. A few weeks before the hearing, Alexandria Ocasio-Cortez, or AOC as she's become known, told me she and her colleagues wanted to visit the border to witness the immigrant detention facilities firsthand. They would go to prepare for the hearings, to testify during them. I was all for it. But I'd told her that our committee couldn't and shouldn't fund their trip. I told her to have her own office and the offices of the other members pay for it, and that way no one could ever accuse the committee of sending them on a mission to gain damning evidence for the hearings.

They did use their own budgets. They went and reported from the border, bringing firsthand accounts of horrific treatment back to Congress and the country. They began telling us that while parents were taken to court and prosecuted, their children were herded into mass, inhumane warehousing facilities, neglected, underfed, under–cared for, and treated like animals. Children were living in cages—often two, three, or more to a cage—with no toilet facilities, no soap, wearing the same clothing day after day. Their mothers were warehoused apart from them, in detention centers, living on six-foot-square pads with aluminum blankets, enduring insults from guards, wondering, worrying, crying over the whereabouts and well-being of the children who had been taken from them.

AOC tweeted from the border:

Now I've seen the inside of these facilities. It's not just the kids. It's everyone. People drinking out of toilets, officers laughing in front of members of Congress. I brought it up to their superiors. They said "officers are under stress & act out sometimes." No accountability.

She sent pictures of people living on small blankets, sharing food, being mocked and treated with disdain by the Border Patrol, the very people supposedly looking out for them.

Tlaib tweeted:

We can't just focus on the children anymore. I met grandmothers, mothers and fathers who are suffering. This is devastating. The look in one father's eyes broke me. I can't look away.

After the tour, she said:

It is my duty as a congresswoman, and an American, to raise hell until immigrants seeking safety and a better life are treated with dignity, respect, and see their human rights protected.

Before the tour began, Congresswoman Ayanna Pressley had stated, "I [am] committed . . . to addressing these human rights violations . . . to getting these children and their families out of incarceration." Afterward she added, "This is about the preservation of our humanity . . . about seeing every single person there as a member of your own family. I am tired of the health and the safety, the humanity, and the full freedoms of Black and Brown children being negotiated and compromised and moderated."

After the tour, at a press conference the congresswomen held, protesters and mobs shouted racist, sexist, vile epithets at them.

"We don't want Muslims here," one person shouted at Tlaib and Omar.

The crowd should have been applauding their bravery and dedication to freedom and democracy, not attacking their heritage. The people in attendance should have been looking inward because every single one of them, without exception, descended from ancestors who came from somewhere else, who came here for a better life, not to be locked up at the border and made to drink from toilets.

The Oversight Committee's first hearings, in July 2019, focused on the child separation policy. Since our new members Ocasio-Cortez, Pressley, and Tlaib were among those who had traveled to the border, they testified as witnesses, along with Texas Democrat Veronica Escobar. All had seen the horrific conditions there. They shared chilling firsthand accounts of children—five, six, seven, ten, and twelve years old—who the Border Patrol had taken away from their parents. These committee members may have been young, but they were powerful. As someone who has mentored a lot of people, I can tell you that my most aggressive colleagues are often the youngest, newest members, the next generation of Democrats. Over and over, I've counseled new members, telling them not to stifle their intentions or purpose, but to use their energy to keep at the task, adding evidence on evidence, witness on witness, act on act. We must do everything we can to put together an ironclad case, a case even a Republican majority in the Senate will have to take seriously. Make a case of behavior that the American people find un-American.

I was right there with them. I understood their outrage and their drive. I shared it.

When we initially began our work, I had no idea how hard it would be to do our job, the lengths the White House would go to in order to prevent the American people from learning the truth—the denials, disregard and disdain for law and justice, suppression of evidence, defiance of subpoenas, twisted facts, attacks on perceived enemies, and outright lies.

But that resistance and obstinance only strengthened my resolve. My life's journey has involved overcoming, setting goals, moving through the obstacles in front of me. Everything I'd accomplished had been building toward this final test, and with the gavel in my hand, the time had come. Our nation had already rebelled against one monarchy— the British—and now, under the Trump administration, we were guarding against another as he and his administration behaved so unethically since the day he took office. I was determined to pursue the actions to oversee and reform his administration. It was long overdue. I was ready.

Something I Can't Stomach

During the hearings that July, the Oversight Committee placed Acting Secretary of the Department of Homeland Security Kevin McAleenan under oath. Among other functions, Homeland Security is responsible for protecting our nation's borders and administering our nation's immigration policies, the rules that govern which immigrants can enter the nation and under what conditions. McAleenan was accountable for telling the truth about the Border Patrol, which reported to him. He had to respond directly to the eyewitness reports, and to me confronting his department and his own personal values.

Since the administration's crackdowns at the border had begun in 2017 and 2018, at least 2,800 children had been separated from their parents. They claimed that efforts were being made to reunite families, but I was skeptical. They acknowledged that in 2019, at least 700 more families had been separated. It was disgraceful. It was disgusting. It was inexcusable. It was almost impossible to hear.

We are better than this!

I knew I had to conduct a fair and unbiased hearing, but when I learned of the abuses, I was sickened and could barely contain my outrage. I have dealt with bad things in my life and career. Crime. Violence. Death. I can deal with the realities of wrongdoing. But the abuse of children is something I cannot stomach.

The department had what they call a "zero tolerance" policy. What it meant was that no one who is technically here illegally or undocumented may enter the country and that in the process of enforcing the policy, children may be separated from parents, no matter the age, illness, or frailty of a child, no matter how far a family has traveled, no matter the political situation they are fleeing, no matter what.

Under this policy, infants can be taken from a nursing mother. Think about that. Zero tolerance. Not strict enforcement, or rigid or firm enforcement, but total and absolute, without allowing for specific conditions or details. No exceptions.

None.

How could one human being treat other human beings like that?

"We hear about stories coming out from you and your agency that everything is pretty good, that you're doing a great job," I said to him as calmly and evenly as I could. "I guess you feel like you're doing a great job. Right?"

He began to answer, "We're doing our level best in a challenging—"

"What does that mean?" I cut in, unable to control myself. "What does that mean when a child is sitting in their own feces, can't take a shower? Come on, man. What is that about? None of us would have our children in that position. They are human beings. . . . I've said it before and I'll say it again, 'It is not the deed you do to a child. It's the memory.' It's the memory. . . . We are the United States of America. We are the greatest country in the world. We are the ones that can go anywhere . . . and save people, make sure they have diapers. Come on. We're better than that."

My voice rose, my face heated, my fists clenched, I looked up to God. I have tried mightily over my career to be a man of calm in a storm, to look for common—or at least not rocky—ground between people, to make friends. Sometimes I have had to fight my inner instincts to do it. Sometimes I fail. That day, at that moment, I vowed, despite my indignation, to cling to my calm.

I expressed my concern that Acting Secretary McAleenan and the administration simply did not feel for other humans. I wondered if they lacked the most basic instinct of sharing the emotions—the pain—of other people.

Did they have an "empathy deficit"?

But the secretary had so little to say, so little in the way of answers. There are no answers to questions about a lack of humanity. To an empathy deficit. I don't even think it was all his fault. The White House, the administration, and his own department put him in that situation. They didn't give him the money or the people to do what had to be done. The administration had provided a godless response. With children in cages, sleeping in feces, torn from their mothers at our borders—God was surely not pleased. God was angry.

An Empathy Deficit

McAleenan's answers, or his lack of answers, were not acceptable or decent. He was accountable for the Border Patrol. That included not only how they were treating children, mothers, fathers, and grandparents, but their own language, attitude, and acts toward us, the U.S. public and their representatives in government, the people looking out for the welfare of these children and families. The people he and his staff actually work for.

Representative Alexandria Ocasio-Cortez questioned him on the actions and attitudes of his staff and what was being done about it.

"Did you see the posts mocking migrant children's deaths?" she asked, referring to inhumane social media posts made by members of the Border Patrol.

"I did," he responded with obvious discomfort.

"Are those officers on the job today and responsible for the safety of migrant women and children?" she interrogated.

Suddenly his responses became unclear as he reverted to bureaucracy-speak.

"[T]here is an aggressive investigation on this issue proceeding," he said, choosing not to answer the question directly.

Ocasio-Cortez asked again, pushing for a straight yes or no answer—"Are these people still on the job?"

"We've already put individuals on administrative duties," the secretary responded, noting that they'd been removed from their normal position and had instead been given a job behind a desk, away from children and families. "I don't know which ones correspond with which posts. And we've issued cease and desist orders to dozens more."

There was one moment in the hearings I actually saw as a good sign—small, but still a signal nonetheless. When pressed on whether separating children and families fosters a "dehumanizing culture"—one that sees some people as less than human, less worthy than others—in his department, the secretary defended the organization.

"We do not have a dehumanizing culture at CBP [Customs and Border Control]. . . . [The department] rescues four thousand people a year" and is "absolutely committed to the well-being of everyone that they interact with."

That answer suggested that McAleenan viewed his job with a glimmer of morality and conscience. He recognized that the department's role was to protect the "well-being" of people. Even if they were failing to carry it out, even if they were crippled by inadequate budgets and manpower, even if they were poisoned by ugly rhetoric from the top of the Trump administration.

In his heart, I don't believe Kevin McAleenan is a bad man. He seems to be an individual who knows what his department is supposed to do. He may be presiding over inhumane acts but he does not seem to excuse them. His sin is that he has not acted to stop them.

I was not surprised when, a few weeks later, he resigned his position.

18

TURN SLOWLY, GRIND FINE

With the Democrats now in the majority, the resolutions to impeach President Donald Trump were gaining steam. The House Oversight Committee went to work. We had a lot to do. And we were determined to do it right. But our first major decision was to wait for Robert Mueller to finish his work.

To remind you, back in May 2017, Mueller started conducting his investigation into the Trump campaign's alleged interference in the 2016 election. His findings would allow us to decide whether impeachment was a viable course. Though we all had serious qualms over the way Trump had handled almost everything, not everyone thought impeachment was the answer. "I'm not for impeachment," Nancy Pelosi had told *The Washington Post*. "Impeachment is so divisive to the country that unless there's something so compelling and overwhelming and bipartisan, I don't think we should go down that path, because it divides the country."

When I took charge of Oversight, Mueller had not yet released his findings. So we simply focused on our plan to investigate, investigate, investigate. Throughout it all, the president unleashed a barrage of inflammatory and bullying tweets. Any and all unfavorable stories about him and his businesses, family, and administration were labeled "fake news."

The Mueller Report was made public in mid-March of 2019. In it, the investigators listed multiple incidents involving Trump that could constitute obstruction of justice. Mueller opted not to accuse the president, but neither he nor his report declared the president innocent of obstruction either. Instead Mueller chose to let Congress make that determination.

The Mueller Report was turned over to the Justice Department and Attorney General William Barr, who jumped the gun by interpreting its conclusions and determining that it did not contain evidence enough to support obstruction of justice. In fact, that was Barr's *opinion* and not the words contained in the report. But given his position as the highest legal officer in the United States, a lot of people took his words to be true. That in itself may turn out to be a violation of duty or law.

Luckily, there were more stones to overturn. The Oversight Committee found itself at the center of that investigation.

Significant and Dangerous

"Raise your right hand. Do you swear or affirm to tell the whole truth and nothing but the truth?"

"I do," said the witness, Michael Cohen, the president's personal lawyer. It was late February 2019 and Cohen was addressing the full Oversight Committee and the world, live and televised. Known as President Trump's "fixer"—the person who handled the president's messes so Trump didn't have to get his own hands dirty—Cohen had already been found guilty of lying to a Senate committee and a number of other crimes. He was appearing on this day because he was willing to tell us exactly how he did what he did on behalf of Donald Trump, during the presidential campaign and after. Oversight precedes reform.

Michael Cohen stood before me, and I was ready to hear what he had to say.

Before he read his prepared statement, I directly addressed the question on everyone's mind: Why should we believe Michael Cohen, a man who lied to Congress and lied to law enforcement about his actions to protect the president? Did this man deserve this moment of redemption?

"Some will certainly ask," I said, "if Mr. Cohen was lying then, why should we believe him now? This is a legitimate question. As a trial lawyer for many years, I've faced this situation over and over again. And I asked the same question. Here is how I view our role. Every one of us in this room has a duty to serve as an independent check on the executive branch. Ladies and gentlemen, we are in search of the truth. The president has made many statements of his own, and now the American people have a right to hear the other side. They can watch Mr. Cohen's testimony and make their own judgment."

I banged the gavel and Michael Cohen addressed the committee and Congress.

"I recognize that some of you may doubt and attack me on my credibility," he said. "It is for this reason that I have incorporated into this opening statement documents that are irrefutable and demonstrate that the information you will hear is accurate and truthful. I am ashamed of my weakness and misplaced loyalty—of the things I did for Mr. Trump in an effort to protect and promote him. I am ashamed because I know what Mr. Trump is. He is a racist. He is a con man. He is a cheat."

To Cohen's credit, he acknowledged the skepticism and then set out to build his case on facts. I may not respect him for what he did in defending Donald Trump all those years, but I recognized a lawyer making a good case.

He started with his own disarming confession.

"Before going further, I want to apologize to each of you and to Congress. . . . The last time I appeared before Congress, I came to protect Mr. Trump. Today, I'm here to tell the truth about Mr. Trump."

He then admitted his own guilt, not broadly or dismissively, but in detail, effectively taking those issues off the table.

"It is painful to admit that I was motivated by ambition at times . . . many times I ignored my conscience and acted loyal to a man when I should not have. . . . I have come here to apologize to my family, to the government, and to the American people."

His tale was as riveting as a Stephen King story; truth is truly stranger than fiction.

Then Cohen described the president of the United States as "fundamentally disloyal." That was a breathtaking phrase. Can the person who holds the position with the highest responsibility in the land be disloyal? To us? To those he represents? To his country? To the Constitution?

Cohen then dissected the president's motives and priorities, dismantling Trump's favorite refrain. "Donald Trump is a man who ran for office to make his brand great, not to make our country great. He never expected to win the primary. He never expected to win the general election. The campaign—for him—was always a marketing opportunity."

Cohen connected the dots between Trump's behavior as a businessman and his White House ethics. "[E]arly on in my work for Mr. Trump he would direct me to lie to further his business interests. . . . I considered it trivial. As the president, I consider it significant and dangerous."

On the subject of Trump's alleged racism, Cohen called upon instances where the president would publicly call poor countries racially disparaging, derogatory names. "In private, he is even worse," Cohen said.

On Trump's financial practices, Cohen provided hard evidence, financial statements—documents that had been almost impossible for us to get.

"Mr. Trump is a cheat. I'm giving the committee today three years of President Trump's financial statements, from 2011 to 2013, which he gave to Deutsche Bank to inquire about a loan to buy the Buffalo Bills."

More evidence. More confession.

Choosing to Tell the Truth

Finally, after so many hours, Michael Cohen ended on a very human, personally vulnerable note. He took ownership of the past, showed remorse for his deeds, and shared that he was afraid for his life. Anyone—Democrat, Republican, independent—any human being could relate to that fear.

"To you, Chairman Cummings [and] the other members of this committee, and the other members of the House and Senate, I am sorry for my lies and for lying to Congress . . . for actively working to hide from you the truth about Mr. Trump when you needed it most. My testimony certainly does not diminish the pain I caused my family and friends. . . . And I have never asked for, nor would I accept, a pardon from President Trump. . . . I am not a perfect man. I have done things I am not proud of, and I will live with the consequences of my actions for the rest of my life. But today, I get to decide the example I set for my children and how I attempt to change how history will remember me. I may not be able to change the past, but I can do right by the American people here today. Thank you."

It was one of the most powerful events I've ever witnessed in my almost seven decades of life. Seven-plus hours of the truth as best as Michael Cohen could recall it.

By the end of the day, I personally had had a transformative experience. The full scope of who and what we were dealing with, which I may have known piece by piece, hit me full force. It was literally staggering.

I saw on the faces of my colleagues, even those who publicly supported the president, that the reality of this man and his values, or vacuum of values, was unprecedented. We had a leader of our country who had no moral center.

It was my job to close the hearing.

I meant my closing words with all of my soul. "When we're dancing with the angels, the question we'll be asked: In 2019, what did we do to make sure we kept our democracy intact? Did we stand on the sidelines and say nothing?"

A Country of Second Chances

I prayed that I would be up to the challenge of finding my voice during what I knew would be one of my life's biggest moments.

"I've listened to all this, and it's very painful," I said. "You made a lot of mistakes, Mr. Cohen—and you've admitted that."

You cannot witness something like his hearing and not feel at least a little for this man, bad as his deeds might have been. Now he'll suffer and so will his family. So I wanted to be empathetic. Being empathetic requires that we think about what it might be like to walk in another person's shoes, even when that makes us uncomfortable. One of the conclusions I reached is that there was more to this man than a confession, an admission. In him I saw the possibility of change. I saw Cohen as a man at a crossroads, like so many I had seen before.

"When I practiced law I represented a lot of lawyers who got in trouble. And you come saying I have made my mistakes, but now I want to change my life," I said to this formerly high-profile attorney. "If we . . . as a nation did not give people an opportunity after they've made mistakes to change their lives, a whole lot of people would not do very well."

I wanted to remind my friends and adversaries in Congress, and anyone and everyone watching, that we are a country of second chances. We were founded as a second chance—so many people forget our history.

I wanted people to look at his deeds and schemes and values in perspective, to refuse and reject and refute them as not us, not America, not who we are.

"We are better than this," I declared to him and to all of us. *"We really are. As a country, we are so much better than this."*

I wanted everyone to declare, "We are better than this," loud and clear, as I did at that moment.

I adjourned the meeting.

19

THE TRAIN STEADILY COMING

It was in August 2019, nearly six months after the Cohen hearings, that I was hospitalized for pneumonia and managed to escape for a few hours to give the speech at the National Press Club. Then a few days after that, the pneumonia cleared and the doctors officially released me. During the next few weeks, I managed to continue doing vital work. I met on the phone with Nancy Pelosi, Adam Schiff, Jerry Nadler, and his staff. I read testimony. I reviewed the impeachment updates. I signed subpoenas.

"Elijah, that's enough for today," Maya would tell me.

"Okay, I'll stop soon," I'd say. Often sheer exhaustion would just force me to close my eyes for a while.

During this time, doctors at Hopkins and NIH monitored the state of my cancer, which had, as they'd suspected, recurred. The question was, could they do anything to slow it down, or limit it. But then my kidneys started to fail. When your kidneys stop working or are working poorly, a procedure called dialysis helps clean the waste and toxins from your blood. I began dialysis visits three times a week.

I relied on a lot of assistance from Maya, and during this period some of my family members helped out, but before long, my dialysis treatments stopped working.

There became—I think the best word is an "inevitability"— to my fate. I knew that we were coming to the end. I didn't know when or how but it was coming, like a train approaching in the distance, when you're not sure how far away it is but you know it is steadily coming toward you.

I began to feel tired, no matter how much rest I got, just tired all the time. I began to experience constant pain, definitely physical, but also emotional and spiritual. The inner me was burning out, so I called Vernon and asked for that second envelope I had given him. I told him to give it to Maya.

At first Vernon told me not to worry about it, that I would rally as I always had.

"I'm tired," I told him. "I'm just so tired. I have to get out of here. I'm too tired."

"Does he mean that he's tired and wants to get out of there, out of the hospital, to go home and rest? Or does he mean something else?" he asked Maya.

"Something else," Maya told him.

Vernon assured me he would give her the envelope.

A day or so later, the doctors came in with some hard news. "The cancer has spread to his upper thigh, gluteal muscles, and into his bones and there is, sadly, nothing more we can do."

No treatments, no procedures, no drug trials, nothing.

I asked to be moved into hospice, where they provide care to keep you comfortable when you are dying. It was time for other people to carry on without me.

Letting Love Speak

On October 17, at 2:30 a.m., Elijah Cummings died at age sixty-eight. His doctors had told him less than forty-eight hours earlier that his cancer had spread throughout his body. There was no more they or anyone could do. Elijah Cummings was moved to hospice for his final hours. During that time, his wife, Maya, was by his bed. She reflected on their life and those last hours.

When Elijah asked to be moved to a hospice, I immediately set about researching facilities in the area. I settled on two and made a field trip in the afternoon to check them out. One was on a hill with trees, inside what looked to be an old mansion. Elijah's first-floor room opened up to a beautiful courtyard with green grass, flowers, and a fountain emitting the soothing sounds of trickling water. I immediately knew that this was the place for Elijah.

When we moved him into the hospice facility at nine that evening, there was no prediction as to how long he might be there, how long he had. Less than six hours later, he was gone. I thought we would have more time to talk, reflect, and say goodbye. I was inconsolable.

Vernon gave me the envelope the next day. Elijah had spelled out everything: the details of his funeral, where it was to be held, who would speak, which suit he wanted to be buried in, what songs should be sung, everything. And I followed it to the letter.

But his family and I wanted him to receive the respect he deserved since he had been so disrespected by Trump in the months leading up to his death. So we worked with Speaker Pelosi's office and staff at the U.S. Capitol to arrange for him to lie in state.

On October 24, 2019, at the National Statuary Hall, Elijah Cummings became the first African American member of Congress to receive that tribute. His casket was draped by a flag and carried by an honor guard of military pallbearers. The choir from Morgan State University, a historically Black university located in Baltimore, sang from the balcony. I stood by his casket. Leaders of both Democrats and Republicans came to give him homage, to pay their last respects.

Senate minority leader Chuck Schumer said, "His authority came not from the office he held, nor from the timbre of his voice. It came from the moral force of his life."

House Speaker Nancy Pelosi called him "our North Star" and "a mentor of the House."

House majority leader Steny Hoyer spoke of him as "a calming influence in a sea of rage" after the Freddie Gray incident.

Republican congressman Mark Meadows talked about their "unexpected" friendship: "for those of us who know Elijah, it is not unexpected or surprising."

Senate majority leader and Republican Mitch McConnell praised him, as others of both parties paid their respects, including Vice President Pence, Attorney General William Barr, former governor of Maryland Martin O'Malley, Baltimore mayor Jack Young, and members of the Congressional Black Caucus, which Elijah had once led.

One day later, on October 25, at the New Psalmist Baptist Church in Baltimore, almost five thousand people gathered—people from the highest offices of government to plain folks from Baltimore neighborhoods, admirers and adversaries, Republicans and Democrats, Black, Brown, and white, old and young, close friends and family and total strangers—any and all who felt the loss of Elijah Cummings. Elijah was honored and received accolades from many, including

Speaker Pelosi; President Clinton; President Obama; Secretary Clinton; former head of the NAACP Kweisi Mfume; staff aide Harry Spikes; Elijah's brother James; his pastor, Bishop Walter Scott Thomas; his daughters, Jennifer and Adia; and me.

I tried to write what I would say but I could not. I thought and I prayed. As Elijah would do, I waited for God to speak to me. I thought about what he would have wanted me to say. When I stood in front of that gathering, the words came. I spoke from my heart, from my soul, about the finest man and most beautiful spirit I have ever known. I let my passion and love for Elijah speak and sing. I said goodbye to my Elijah.

The Remaining Goal

In those last days of his illness, events had moved toward impeachment at blinding speed. As if sped by his passing, the circumstances moved even faster in the days just after his death.

On December 18, 2019, Speaker Nancy Pelosi banged the gavel and announced that the House of Representatives voted 230 to 197 to impeach President Donald J. Trump, the third president in the history of the United States to face impeachment charges.

That evening, during her press conference, she spoke about Elijah, saying that he "isn't with us physically in this room, but I know [he] is present, was present all day for the deliberations." She honored him as a key force in the inquiry, "our North Star," as she had called him. And she quoted him, "When the history books are written about this tumultuous era, I want them to show that I was among those in the House of Representatives who stood up to lawlessness and tyranny." She added, "He also said, somewhat presciently, 'When we're dancing with angels, the question will be, "What did you do to make sure we kept our democracy intact?"'" We did all we could, Elijah. We passed the two articles of impeachment. The president is impeached."

As the year neared its end, on December 28, 2019, *The Baltimore Sun* named Elijah Cummings the Person of the Year in Maryland. The editorial board's recognition referred to Elijah's words from the hearing in February, again: "'When we're dancing with the angels, the question will be asked: In 2019, what did we do to make sure we kept our democracy intact? Did we stand on the sidelines and say nothing?'" The *Sun* story concluded, "Though he couldn't have known the angels would come for him before the year was out, Elijah Cummings certainly must have been secure in the knowledge that he did all he could to stand up for his beliefs. We are."

A day later, in their year-end feature "The Lives They Lived," *The New York Times Magazine* recognized a select group of "artists, innovators, and thinkers we lost in the past year." The writer who penned the profile of Elijah, Astead

Herndon, concluded with these words: "He always knew that democracy and racism were ideas in direct conflict, and that perfecting one required overcoming the other."

Led by the House clerk and the House sergeant at arms, two weeks into the new year, on January 15, 2020, Nancy Pelosi and the managers formally presented the articles of impeachment to the secretary of the Senate. It was a little more than one year from the date that Elijah became chair of the Oversight and Reform Committee of the House of Representatives.

Oversight had been carried out. Reform was the remaining goal.

So much of this had begun with Elijah's work—the hearings and investigations of the Oversight Committee, the testimony of Trump's personal attorney/fixer Michael Cohen, subpoenas for White House documents and financial records, court cases to compel cooperation where the administration had been stonewalling, the stirring, inspiring, passionate words to Congress and the country, and the promises to our children. It was both heartening and saddening to see the dedication and effectiveness of his work, but knowing he would never see it come to fruition. That made my decision to carry on for him only stronger. With every transgression, every disregard for the Constitution, every attempt to act above the law, I could hear Elijah's voice: "We're better than this. We're better than this."

Yes, we are. We must be.

FAREWELL TO ELIJAH CUMMINGS

Selected Excerpts of Eulogies for Elijah Cummings

BISHOP WALTER SCOTT THOMAS
—Elijah's Pastor

Elijah was my friend for almost forty years. He sat right over there. . . . Elijah's last official congressional act was to sign some subpoenas. I saw him that morning, I did not know he was still working but he was. But that was not his last official act for God. . . . Elijah's last official act for the kingdom of God was to bring power to church. . . . His last official act [takes] place today. . . . The decision was made by his wife that his service would be in one place, the New Psalmist Baptist Church. And he was bringing power to church.

. . . He would be the first to tell you he wasn't perfect . . . that he struggled and wrestled like everybody else . . . that he had to climb the rough side of the mountain. . . . Elijah said I come to church because . . . He looks beyond my faults and God sees my needs. . . . I come to church because I can recognize my failures and I can claim my possibilities so that when I leave . . . I can go out of here and help somebody else.

. . . Elijah brought you to church today so that the moral compass can be reset, so you can get your grounding back, so we can remember "We hold these truths to be self-evident, that all men are created equal and are endowed by their creator with certain inalienable rights of which are life, liberty, and the pursuit of happiness."

. . . Elijah never forgot his grounding. Elijah was like the prophet Elijah . . . according to an Old Testament scholar . . . Elijah's voice would rise, his lips would quiver, he would say "Come on now, we can do better than this." Elijah said as long as God gives me breath, I will speak for those who cannot speak.

. . . Sleep on Elijah, sleep on. It took me a while to get here but I can stand before my God and I can hear him say, well done.

HILLARY CLINTON
—Former Secretary of State

It is no coincidence, is it, that Elijah Cummings shared a name with an Old Testament prophet, whose name, in Hebrew, is "the Lord is my God" . . . who used the power and the wisdom that God gave him to uphold the moral law that all people are subject to. And because all people are equal, like the prophet, our Elijah could call down fire from heaven. But he also prayed and worked for healing. He weathered storms and earthquakes, but never lost his faith. Like that Old Testament prophet, he stood against corrupt leadership of King Ahab and Queen Jezebel, and he looked out for the vulnerable among us. . . . And he kept reminding us . . . the American people want to live their lives without fear of their leaders.

Elijah often said his philosophy was simple: do something, go out and do something. No matter how daunting a problem seems, no matter how helpless you feel, surely there is something you can do. You can defend the truth, you can defend democracy, you can lift up others.

Toward the end of his life he said, "I am begging the American people to pay attention to what is going on, because if you want to have a democracy intact for your children and your children's children and generations yet unborn, we have got to guard this moment. This is our watch."

NANCY PELOSI
—Speaker of the House

Elijah Cummings [was] the first African American lawmaker ever to lie in repose in the Capitol of the United States. Elijah brought people together in life of different parties and in his death of different parties.

. . . As we know from the Old Testament, there is a tradition to leave a seat at the table for Elijah, who might show up, but our Elijah always made a seat at the table for others. He made a seat at the table for children who needed an education, for even new members of Congress so that he could mentor them, for all who wanted to be part of the American dream.

. . . God truly blessed America with the life and legacy of Elijah E. Cummings, mentor, master of the house, North Star, Mr. Chairman, master of the house. May he rest in peace, Elijah Cummings.

KWEISI MFUME
—Former Head of the NAACP

Elijah and I spent a lot of time in the last couple of years privately just talking about our own lives, our own death . . . our own mortality, our own funerals. Whether he was going to go before me or I was going to go before him. [I'd say] because I was three years older than Elijah . . . I will probably be leaving before you. And he would say . . . I hear they're all filled up downstairs, where you're going—where you're going, you may have to get in line.

Sometimes out of the blue, he would call me and just speak [and say] . . . you have turned forty. Of course, Elijah was thirty-seven. Like [when I] turned sixty and of course, he was fifty-seven. . . . Yesterday was my birthday and I did not hear from my friend Elijah.

. . . My preference would be for Elijah to be standing here right now, talking and speaking about me.

JENNIFER CUMMINGS
—Elijah's Older Daughter

Daddy . . . here's a letter to express my gratitude to you for a lifetime of lessons, and memories and blessings. Dear Dad . . . while you were congressman and Mr. Chairman and a seasoned political leader, perhaps the most important title you held in your sixty-eight years of life on this earth was "Dad."

Thank you for loving me before I even took my first breath in this world. I remember you telling me how when I was born, you were amazed you could hold me in the palm of your hand—just one hand, my life in your hands.

Thank you for teaching me the dual power of my beauty and my brilliance. This might sound boastful . . . but ever since I was a little girl, my dad always told me I was beautiful.

Dad wanted me to understand and appreciate my blackness. And truly feel that my rich brown skin was just as beautiful as alabaster or any shade of the rainbow. . . . So I could truly appreciate myself and what may be different, from the width of my nose to the fullness of my lips and the coarseness of my hair. I vividly remember being on the playground . . . a classmate called me ugly. . . . I retorted, "Well, my daddy says I'm beautiful."

. . . Thank you Dad, for . . . teaching me to be bold and confident . . . to stand up against bullies. . . . Thanks for teaching me what leadership means. Thank you for teaching me to persevere.

. . . I will miss our brief conversations between meetings and hearings. And I will miss our longer ones. Our conversations will not be in person anymore, but they will be just as they have always been—filled with spirit and soul. I love you, Dad.

ADIA CUMMINGS
—Elijah's Younger Daughter

You will all have to forgive me, I am reading off of my phone. I am a millennial.

. . . I [want] to share a glimpse of what it was like to be his daughter. My dad protected me, sometimes to tell me he was proud of me or to give me words of encouragement. Whenever I called, his voice answered, "Hey, beautiful." And I could tell he was happy to hear from me. He was never hesitant to give me his opinion whether I asked for it or not. He was quick to remind me that I owed him some money. He wasn't a father known for patience, but rather for persistence. When I was getting ready to take my driving test, he made me parallel park it felt like fifty times in a row . . . until I got it down to a science. I passed the test on the first try.

. . . Last year, I gave him a card for Father's Day. It said, "It's a parent's job to see the child the way God sees them" and you do that for me. I would encourage all of the parents here and watching to see their children the way my dad saw me, in the way God sees me—without limitation, not bound by obstacles or circumstances and with power to determine my own destiny.

JAMES CUMMINGS
—Elijah's Brother

Elijah was my older brother by three years. I can tell you . . . at times it was easy, and at other times it was not. I followed him into middle school and the teachers expected so much of me. When it came time for high school . . . he wanted me to go to City College [high school]. He said . . . it's an all-boys' school so you'll have no distraction. I said, "But I love distractions."

. . . Elijah . . . [always] wanted to be in a position to help the people who could not help themselves. . . . I want to thank each and every one of you [for coming]. You can give someone your car, let them borrow it, or your homes, or whatever the case may be. The one thing you cannot get back is time. Each and every one of you have given up hours of your time to honor my brother. And for that I am eternally grateful.

HARRY SPIKES
—Congressional Staff/District Director

The remarks that I will give to you today are entitled "The Final Lesson."

The congressman asked me [to help him out for] one day in D.C. . . . Little did I know that this will turn into . . . years of working with an angel. Suddenly my life changed from District Director to bodyguard, mechanic, advisor, driver, chef . . . most importantly, friend. . . . He always took time to teach me and the staff valuable life lessons.

Lesson number one: compassion and kindness. He taught me that compassion and kindness brought us closer to God . . . the keys to uniting the human spirit.

Lesson number two: the congressman believed in bridges . . . that an opportunity, no matter how big or small, made the difference between life or death.

Lesson number three: value your friendships. Be the foundation for your friends when the house collapses, be the roof for your friends when rain comes.

Lesson number four: . . . a true leader, to get the ball down the court, to win, shares the ball. Give others the opportunity to lead.

Lesson number five: work through your pain. . . . When we traveled the country, his mission was to fight for the soul of democracy . . . he was always in pain. However, when it was time to address his audience, the congressman transformed into a spiritual warrior.

For days I've been trying to figure out the final lesson. But I finally got it. The congressman would tell me, Harry, remember to be greater than your pain. Continue to fight when all hope is lost. . . . If one leg doesn't work, use a walker, at least you will be standing. . . . [R]emember the final lesson—life may change; you may change; hard choices will come. But the congressman proved to us all that courage and will are timeless.

MAYA CUMMINGS
—Elijah's Wife

This man lived for God and he is of God. I have come here today to say two simple words: Thank you. Thank you. . . .

I want you all to know that . . . what Congressman, Chairman Cummings did was not easy. And it got infinitely more difficult in the last months of his life. When he sustained personal attacks and attacks on his beloved city. While he carried himself with grace and dignity in all public forums . . . it hurt him. He was a man of soul and spirit. He felt very deeply. He was very empathetic. It was one of his greatest gifts . . . his ability to be a public servant, and a man of the people.

. . . [I]t wasn't easy in the last months of his life because he absolutely was in pain. But he was a walking miracle. Do you know that he was diagnosed with a life-threatening illness more than twenty-five years ago? He was given six months to live more than twenty-five years ago!

. . . It was my distinct honor and privilege to be his spouse. Just two days before he died, he was in a lot of pain. He could no longer walk. And he kept saying, "I'm tired. I'm ready to go."

. . . [T]he wonderful world-class staff at the Johns Hopkins Hospital . . . said that they wanted to give him sunshine therapy . . . so they rolled his entire medical bed out of the room onto the rooftop of Johns Hopkins Hospital. Everywhere the sun was shining, and it was just absolutely glorious.

It was God's day. . . . [H]e looked out over the Inner Harbor, Harbor East; he looked toward South Baltimore, his beloved South Baltimore, where he grew up in his early years; he looked toward the downtown; and he looked toward the west side and he said, "Boy, have I come a long way."

And he absolutely came a long way.

. . . Thank you for allowing him to serve you because it was his greatest honor and privilege to work on behalf of all of you.

BILL CLINTON
—Forty-second President

Almost exactly twenty-one years ago Elijah invited me here [to his church] on the Sunday before the election. If you're president, your staff is always trying to tell you why you shouldn't do something. . . . My staff said, I get why you want to go to an African American church, but why would you want to go to Baltimore—they always vote for you. Why would you go for Elijah Cummings . . . he literally hadn't finished one term yet. . . . I said, I get the feeling this is something we ought to do. I got to listen to Elijah that day . . . his quiet reasoned voice, going into his booming voice—"They who wait upon the Lord will have their strength renewed with wings as eagles."

I've had a lot of chances to think about . . . Elijah's lasting legacy to us. We should think again about the prophet Elijah. He was about to be killed for . . . his faith. [At] Mount Sinai, he received a message from God. Go up and stand on top of the mountain and wait for the voice of God. . . . And a huge wind came . . . then an earthquake . . . then the fire came. Then what does the scripture say—"A still small voice." We should hear Elijah now in the quiet times . . . when we need courage . . . and don't know if we believe anymore. Let our Elijah be for us "a still small voice" that keeps us going. . . .

BARACK OBAMA
—Forty-fourth President

The Parable of the Sower . . . tells us . . . [of] those with a noble and good heart, who hear the word, retain it, and by persevering produce a crop. Elijah Cummings came from good sowers and . . . goodness took root.

. . . His parents were sharecroppers from the South, then sought something better in this city. . . . Robert worked shifts at a plant and Ruth cleaned other people's homes. They became parents of seven, preachers to a small flock. I had the pleasure of meeting Elijah's mother and she told me she prayed for me every day, and I knew it was true. And I felt better for it. Sometimes people say they're praying for you, and you don't know. They might be praying about you, but you don't know if they're praying for you.

Elijah's example: the son of parents who rose from nothing to carve out just a little something. The public servant who toiled to guarantee the least of us have the same opportunities that he had earned. . . . That's why he fought for justice. . . . That's why he went on to fight for the rights and opportunities of forgotten people all across America, not just in his district.

. . . It's been remarked that Elijah was a kind man. . . . I want my daughters to know . . . that being a strong man includes being kind. That there's nothing weak about kindness and compassion. There's nothing weak about looking out for others. There's nothing weak about being honorable.

. . . [T]he "honorable" Elijah E. Cummings . . . this is a title that we confer on all kinds of people who get elected to public office . . . but Elijah Cummings was honorable before he was elected to office. There's a difference. There's a difference if you were honorable and treated others honorably outside the limelight, on the side of a road, in a quiet moment counseling somebody you work with, letting your daughters know you love them. As president, I knew I could always count on Elijah being honorable and doing the right thing. And people have talked about his voice. There is something about his voice. . . . I would watch Elijah rally his colleagues. "The cost of doing nothing isn't nothing," he would say, and folks would remember why they entered into public service.

. . . "Our children are the living messages we send to a future we will never see," he would say, and he would remind all of us that our time is too short not to fight for what's good and what is true and what is best in America. Elijah Cummings was a man of noble and good heart. His parents and his faith planted the seeds of hope and love and compassion and the righteousness and that good soil of his. He has harvested all the crops that he could, for the Lord has now called Elijah home to give His humble, faithful servant rest.